HIS CALLING DISCIPLESHIP

FOR THE NEW BELIEVER

JOHN ONORATO

Printed in the USA

ISBN 979-8-218-48579-5

BIBLIOGRAPHY

(n.d.). *New King James Version.* Bible Hub. Retrieved May 30, 2024, from https://biblehub.com/nkjv

(n.d.). *New Revised Standard Version Catholic Edition.* Bible Gateway. Retrieved May 30, 2024, from https://www.biblegateway.com

(n.d.). English Standard Version. Bible Hub. Retrieved May 30, 2024, from https://biblehub.com/esv

(n.d.). *Christian Standard Bible.* Bible Hub. Retrieved May 30, 2024, from https://biblehub.com/csb

(n.d.). *Holman Christian Standard Bible.* Bible Gateway. Retrieved May 30, 2024, from https://www.biblegateway.com

(n.d.). *King James Version.* Bible Gateway. Retrieved May 30, 2024, from https://www.biblegateway.com

(n.d.). *The Message.* Bible Gateway. Retrieved May 30, 2024, from https://www.biblegateway.com

(n.d.). *Strong's Lexicon.* Bible Gateway. Retrieved May 30, 2024, from https://www.biblegateway.com

(n.d.). *New International Version.* Bible Hub. Retrieved May 30, 2024, from https://biblehub.com/niv

(n.d.). *New Living Translation.* Bible Gateway. Retrieved May 30, 2024, from https://www.biblegateway.com

(n.d.). *New American Bible Revised Edition.* Bible Gateway. Retrieved May 30, 2024, from https://www.biblegateway.com

This book is dedicated to:

Every pre-Christian and new believer that wants to get to know God better. I'm thrilled to introduce you to my loving God and Father that has been calling you since birth. This book is not a substitute for joining with a local body of believers but is the guide I wish I had when I was starting my journey as a child of God.

CONTENTS

PREFACE

I was Catholic for 20 years, Methodist for 20 years, and Baptist for 10 years. Since then, I've been an independent or nondenominational Christian. I love all the denominations and pray for unity among them. I also pray for a Holy Christian Church where differences are minimized, and the love of God and others is maximized. I have found that the most significant difference between denominations is "worship style" and "man-made doctrinal rules." This book intends to bring truth found in Scripture to discipleship training. It is designed to be used in any Christian denomination where God the Father, Son, and Holy Spirit are exalted.

As I look back on my Christian education; as a child and youth in Catechism, in Sunday school, then as a teacher of denominational Sunday schools and a seminary student for ten years, now with a Master of Divinity, I have unpacked my beliefs several times and searched the Scriptures for truth before packing them back up in my mind. I will show you things I found in Scripture that I wish others had shown me early in my Christian education. The purpose of this book is not intended to serve as a comprehensive systematic theology but will provide you with a basic Biblical foundation of the Gospel of Jesus Christ.

Many people say that the Bible is the "Word of God" (and it is), but the Word of God is also a person, and that person is Jesus Christ. So, whether you're talking about the Bible or Jesus, "the Word" always points us back toward God.

I took a world religion class in seminary where I studied and interviewed people with beliefs from other world religions: Judaism, Hinduism, Islam, Buddhism, Sikhism, etc. The main difference between all world religions and Christianity is that only in Christianity, God comes to live in the believer. In all other religions, one follows the Law that identifies sin and keeps people in shame, guilt, and condemnation. In other world religions, people are always trying to work their way into right standing with God, and it's never known when one is "good enough" to receive eternal life in heaven or nirvana or reincarnation. All other world religions base Salvation on one's goodness and good works as they search for God's blessing. Christianity is not based on your performance or what you do but on what Jesus did for us. In Christianity, you are saved by faith and grace.

In Christianity, Jesus paid the price. We wear his Righteousness. We are made right with God through His works and not our efforts. When you accept Jesus as Savior, your eternal life is secured in heaven. There is nothing you can do to take yourself out from under the grace of God through Christ. If you are a believing Christian, God the Father, Son, and Holy Spirit come to make their home in you. Jesus paid the price once and for all the sins of the World, past, present, and future. Those who receive him as Lord and Savior become heirs of God and co-heirs with Christ **(Romans 8:17)**. This is the foundation for the Gospel of Jesus Christ, given to us in the New Testament. Other religions are searching for God but in Christianity, God came searching for you. That's the good news!

This book will help you to discover, know, and do the will of God. What good is it if someone picks up an exercise manual and studies it in all its languages, versions, and translations but never uses what they've learned? Unfortunately, that's the life of many Christians today. Unless you are walking out the great commission, you are not going about "Father's business." Many think doing administration, being on the worship team or preparing the sanctuary for service is doing "Father's business," but Jesus never said, "Go into all the world and keep the churches clean." Someone needs to clean the church, but even the janitor is called to spread the Gospel, lead people to the Lord, get people healed, make disciples, and be Jesus to the World!

In this writing, I hope you find new life, freedom, and power in Christ. The Scriptures contained herein will illuminate God's plan for your life no matter what denomination, age, stage, income level, or job you have. Your new identity will lead you into a deeper relationship with God, who desires an abundant life for you!

God didn't just come to give you eternal life in heaven. He also came to restore you to an intimate relationship with Himself, be your guide in life through the Holy Spirit, and bless you with an inheritance of all the riches and power of the kingdom of God now and forever. Blessings on your journey through this book!

John Onorato - MDiv
His Calling Ministries

John 10:10 NKJV "The thief does not come except to steal, and to kill, and to destroy. I have come that they may have life and that they may have it more abundantly."

Note: This book is written as a study guide for the new believer. It is intended to be used in conjunction with a Bible. A New Living Translation Study Bible that you can also highlight and write your thoughts in is suggested. If you can't write on the pages of your current Bible buy one that you can write in. A Bible app on your electronic device will also suffice.

There are spaces in each section to write your thoughts and to look up and write key Bible verses. Writing is the best way to retain information. In case you don't have access to a Bible, the referenced Scriptures are included at the end of each chapter. Each section is designed for reading, writing and reflection. I hope you enjoy your journey with God's word through this book and the Holy Spirit as your guide.

LESSON 1.1

SIN, SALVATION, and ETERNAL LIFE

The primary message of the Bible is God's plan of Salvation, deliverance, healing, and wholeness. God created us to have a relationship with Him. Scripture shows us how sin destroyed that relationship over and over again. God sent Jesus to restore that relationship. Those who accept Jesus as Lord and Savior are restored to a right relationship with God. This truth is the starting point for understanding the Bible and God's plan and purpose for your life.

John 3:16 NKJV

____

____

____

____

Many think Salvation leads to eternal life. As human beings, we are already immortal. Our physical body will die, but our soul and spirit will live on eternally.

Ecclesiastes 12:7 NKJV "Then the dust will return to the earth as it was, and the spirit will return to God who gave it."

Everyone, whether a believer or unbeliever, will continue to live for eternity somewhere. The only question is where that will be.

1 John 5:11-12 NKJV "And this is the testimony: That God has given us eternal life, and this life is in His Son. He who has the Son has life; he who does not have the Son of God does not have life."

Jesus didn't just come so that you would have eternal life with Him in heaven after death. He came so that you could have an intimate and personal relationship with the Father, Son, and Holy Ghost now. That's Good News!

John 17:3 NKJV "This is eternal life, that they may know You, the only true God, and Jesus Christ whom You have sent."

2 Corinthians 6:18 NIV "I will be a Father to you, and you will be my sons and daughters, says the Lord Almighty."

Satan seeks to destroy your relationship with God through sin, but he has no power today except what he had from the very beginning. He tempts us through lies and deception.

John 8:44 NKJV (Jesus speaking to unbelievers) "You belong to your Father, the devil, and you want to carry out your Father's desires. He was a murderer from the beginning, not holding to the truth, for there is no truth in him. When he lies, he speaks his native language, for he is a liar and the Father of lies."

1 Peter 5:8-9 NKJV "Be sober, be vigilant; because your adversary the devil walks about like a roaring lion, seeking whom he may devour. Resist him, steadfast in the faith, knowing that the same sufferings are experienced by your brotherhood in the World."

MEMORIZATION VERSE

1 Corinthians 10:13 NKJV

____

____

____

____

Note: Blanks are for you to write the key verses. Writing improves memorization. Find them in your Bible (ap) or at the end of each chapter.

Revelation 21:27 NIV "Nothing impure will ever enter it (heaven), nor will anyone who does what is shameful or deceitful, but only those whose names are written in the Lamb's book of life."

Romans 6:23 NKJV "For the wages of sin is death, but the gift of God is eternal life in Christ Jesus our Lord."

John 3:2 NKJV "Jesus answered and said to him, "Most assuredly, I say to you, unless one is born again, he cannot see the kingdom of God."

Romans 10:9 NKJV

____

____

____

____

No one goes to heaven by doing good works or being good. Being moral, ethical, attending church, giving to the poor, or being kind to others does not grant you entrance into heaven. These are all good things, but this is where most people get it wrong. Jesus saves by faith through grace, not by your performance. Jesus says this several times, but most succinctly in **Ephesians 2:8-9.**

Ephesians 2:8-9 NIV "For it is by grace you have been saved, through faith and this is not from yourselves. It is the gift of God, not by works, so that no one can boast."

Works come from loving God not from trying to earn God's love.

1 John 4:19 KJV "We love him, because he first loved us."

PERSONAL REFLECTION:
HOW IS HOLY SPIRIT SPEAKING TO YOU THROUGH THESE SCRIPTURES?

____

____

____

____

Sin keeps the unbeliever from being part of God's family **(Galatians 5:19-21)** Any sin; lying, cheating, swearing, stealing, fighting, evil thoughts, etc., but Jesus paid for your sins at the cross in order to restore God's original plan of Salvation and relationship with Him.

We get to be part of God's family in heaven and live a victorious, abundant life in an intimate relationship with God by the grace of Jesus Christ and faith in him.

Ask Jesus into your life and believe in your heart, and you will be saved.

PRAYER OF SALVATION

Jesus, I am a sinner, and I need a Savior. Thank You for dying on the cross for my sins. I receive you today as my Lord and Savior. Thank You forforgiving my sins, making me part of God's family, and giving me eternal life. Write my name in the Lamb's Book of Life and fill me with the Holy Spirit. Take control of my life and make me the person You want me to be.

Amen

If this prayer is from your heart, you have become part of God's family, and your Salvation is secured for eternity. God no longer holds your sins against you. That's the Good News! You have a new Father in Heaven and new brothers and sisters on earth. When someone asks you what makes you a Christian, your answer now is, "Jesus is my Lord and Savior!"

ANSWER KEY: LESSON 1.1: SIN, SALVATION, AND ETERNAL LIFE

John 3:16 NKJV "For God so loved the world that He gave His only begotten Son, that whoever believes in Him should not perish but have everlasting life."

Q1 Who is eligible for everlasting life with God in Heaven?
Everyone that accepts Jesus as Lord and Savior.

Q2 When does eternal life begin and end?
It begins when we are born. It never ends. We are eternal beings from birth.

MEMORIZATION VERSE

1 Corinthians 10:13 NKJV "No temptation has overtaken you except what is common to mankind. And God is faithful; he will not let you be tempted beyond what you can bar. But when you are tempted, he will also provide a way out so that you can endure it."

Romans 10:9 NKJV "If you confess with your mouth that Jesus is Lord and believe in your heart that God has raised Him from the dead, you will be saved."

Galatians 5:19-21 NKJV "Now the works of the flesh are evident, which are: adultery, fornication, uncleanness, lewdness, idolatry, sorcery, hatred, contentions, jealousies, outbursts of wrath, selfish ambitions, dissensions, heresies, envy, murders, drunkenness, revelries, and the like; of which I tell you beforehand, just as I also told *you* in time past, that those who practice such things will not inherit the kingdom of God."

LESSON 1.2

IDENTITY IN CHRIST

You have a new identity in Christ starting now! This identity is the foundation of operating in the Kingdom of God in power on the earth. **(1 Corinthians 2:4).** You are now a child of God. You are a new spiritual creature/creation, and your home is in heaven.

John 1:12 NKJV "Yet to all who did receive him, to those who believed in His name he gave the right to become children of God."

2 Corinthians 5:17 KJV "If anyone is in Christ, he is a new creature/creation; old things have passed away; behold, all things have become new."

You live in the World, but you are no longer of it. You are a 3-part person. You are born-again (Spirit), with a mind and emotions (soul), living in a body. (Spirit, Soul, and Body). Let's look at these claims in Scripture.

1 Thessalonians 5:23 NLT "Now may the God of peace make you holy in every way, and may your whole spirit, soul, and body be kept blameless until our Lord Jesus Christ comes again."

Now that you're a "born-again believer," sin has been eradicated from your life forever. How many sins did you commit "after" Jesus died on the cross? All of them! Therefore, Jesus took care of every sin, past, present, and future, at the cross. You are no longer a "sinner" or a "sinner saved by grace." You are now a new creation.

Romans 6:6 NIV "For we know that our old self was crucified with him so that the body ruled by sin might be done away with, that we should no longer be slaves to sin."

John 17:16 NIV "They are not of the world, even as I am not of the world."

Chapter 3 will cover renewing your soul/mind in more detail. For now, know that God has come to live in you, and your new identity is IN HIM.

God lives in the believer. Jesus lives in the believer, and Holy Spirit lives in the believer. He is in you, and you are IN HIM. For further study, there are over 100 verses in the New Testament that describe our position "in Him", "in Christ", and "in Jesus." An online concordance is helpful for finding these and all biblical word and phrase searches.

MEMORIZATION VERSE: ACTS 17:28 NKJV

____

____

____

____

1 John 4:15 NKJV "Whoever confesses that Jesus is the Son of God, God abides in him, and he in God."

John 14:20 NKJV "At that day you will know that I am in My Father, and you in Me, and I in you."

2 Corinthians 13:5 NKJV "Do you not know yourselves, that Jesus Christ is in you?"

When you are "born again" (at the time you accept Jesus as Lord and Savior/Salvation), you are baptized in the Holy Spirit meaning, Jesus puts His Holy Spirit IN YOU!

Romans 8:11 NKJV "If the Spirit of Him who raised Jesus from the dead dwells in you, He who raised Christ from the dead will also give life to your mortal bodies through His Spirit who dwells in you."

John 15:19-20 NKJV "Then Jesus answered and said to them, "Most assuredly, I say to you, the Son can do nothing of Himself, but what He sees the Father do; for whatever He does, the Son also does in like manner. For the Father loves the Son, and shows Him all things that He does; and He will show Him greater works than these, that you may marvel."

Why did Jesus say, "the Son can do nothing of Himself?"

Philippians 2:7 NLT

____

____

____

____

In other words, even though he was fully God, he chose to act only within the power given to all human beings who possess the Holy Spirit. Acting only as a human being, he "could do nothing of himself," but through the power of the Holy Spirit, he showed what is possible for all human beings to do. He demonstrated this throughout his ministry. (Heal the sick, raise the dead, and cast out demons.) Then he not only tells us to do these things by the power of the Holy Spirit which He has given us, but he raises the bar and says the following:

John 14:12 NLT "I tell you the truth, anyone who believes in me will do the same works I have done, and even greater works, because I am going to be with the Father."

John 15:19-20 (above) should give us great comfort. Jesus says that He only said and did what he heard the Father saying and doing.

Then, in **John 16:13**, he says the Holy Spirit only says and does what he hears and sees Jesus saying and doing.

John 16:13 NKJV "However, when He, the Spirit of truth, has come, (Holy Spirit) He will guide you into all truth; for He will not speak on His own authority, but whatever He hears (from Jesus) He will speak; and He will tell you things to come."

"God the Holy Spirit" tells you what he hears from "God the Son" (Jesus), who tells you what he hears from "God the Father." All of whom have made their home in you. His identity is IN YOU, and your new identity is IN HIM. This reality is what it means to be a Christian. You are the body of Christ. You represent Jesus to the World because he lives in you, and nothing can take you out of God's hands.

John 10:29-30 NKJV "My Father, who has given them to Me, is greater than all; and no one can snatch them out of my Father's hand. I and my Father are one."

Romans 8:38 NKJV "I am persuaded that neither death nor life, nor angels nor principalities nor powers, nor things present nor things to come, nor height nor depth, nor any other created thing, shall be able to separate us from the love of God which is in Christ Jesus our Lord."

You are a new creation. Your new identity and purpose in life are found in Jesus Christ. You are a child of God, loved by the Father, and forgiven forever for all past, present, and future sins. You were designed to be in fellowship with God and created to reflect His glory as you walk through life, reflecting His love and carrying out His will.

Romans 8:14-17 NKJV "For as many as are led by the Spirit of God, these are sons of God. For you did not receive the Spirit of bondage again to fear, but you received the Spirit of adoption by whom we cry out, "Abba," "Father." The Spirit Himself bears witness with our Spirit that we are children of God, and if children, then heirs of God and joint heirs with Christ."

How do you know if you are NOT living out God's will or purpose for your life?

1. If sin controls your life, you are not living according to God's will or purpose for your life.
2. If you wake up each day with apathy or boredom, or if no one comes to Christ through your example, you might not be living out God's plan.
3. Do you describe yourself by what you do for work, your position, or a performance achievement?
4. Do you identify yourself by income, social circles, things you own, or the way you look?
5. Are you sharing the Gospel?
6. Are you in a place of Christian service to others?

Satan's greatest lie suggests you could form your identity through things of the World. Since the beginning of creation, people have tried to fill their identities with achievements or performance. Their personal history, family lineage, social circles, and sexual desires are all self-made identities and idols that fall short of the new creation God made them to be.

Because of our new identity in Christ, we now stand righteous and uncondemned before God. He gave us His

1. Righteousness (living in right relationship with God and others),
2. Holiness (being set apart fo things things of God),
3. Redemption (the work of Christ on our behalf),

4. Wisdom (God's perspective to apply truth for Godly ends)
5. Justification (you are no longer guilty of sin), and
6. Sanctification (you are Holy and set apart for God's use).

Romans 8:1 NKJV

____

____

____

____

In your new identity, you are a new creation. You are forgiven, purified, and a child of God. You have a new Father in Heaven.

Meditate on your new identity. "He's in me, I'm in Him, and we are one!"

PERSONAL REFLECTION:

HOW IS HOLY SPIRIT SPEAKING TO YOU THROUGH THESE SCRIPTURES?

____

____

____

____

ANSWER KEY: LESSON 1.2: IDENTITY IN CHRIST

1 Corinthians 2:4 NKJV " My speech and my preaching *were* not with persuasive words of human wisdom, but in demonstration of the Spirit and of power."

MEMORIZATION VERSE

Acts 17:28 NKJV "In Him we live and move and have our being, as some of your own poets have said, for we are also His offspring."

Philippians 2:7 NLT "He gave up his divine privileges; he took the humble position of a slave/servant and was born as a human being."

Romans 8:1 NKJV "There is therefore now no condemnation for those who are in Christ Jesus."

LESSON 2.1

LAW and GRACE

The most critical teaching left out of most Christian Institutions of higher learning and churches today, is the issue of Law and Grace. Study the Scripture on this, and you will be able to rightly divide Old Testament (Jewish) law, which keeps you under shame, guilt, and condemnation, from the New Testament Gospel of Grace, which comes from the unmerited favor of God and the finished work of Jesus Christ.

2 Timothy 2:15 NKJV "Be diligent to present yourself approved to God, a worker who does not need to be ashamed, rightly dividing the word of truth."

Simply put, the Old Testament put people under the Law. The Ten Commandments became 613 Jewish commandments under the weight of which no one could be made right with God. Therefore, the blood of unblemished animals was sacrificed to atone for sin. This sacrifice was temporary and had to be performed annually.

Jesus came and fulfilled all the Law. He completed all the work he set out to do. By His shed blood he became the permanent sacrifice. He Redeemed humanity from the curse of the law. He restored dominion over the earth to those that believe in Him. He nailed the law to the cross. He paid the price for the sins of the World and proclaimed all these things to be finished.

Colossians 2:14 NIV "Having canceled the charge of our legal indebtedness, which stood against us and condemned us; he has taken it away, nailing it to the cross."

John 19:30 NIV "When he had received the drink, Jesus said, "It is finished." With that, he bowed his head and gave up his spirit."

When he rose from the dead a New Testament of grace came into effect. Beginning with His resurrection, we see a New Testament no longer constructed from religion, legalism, or performance based on the Law.

So, to rightly divide the Scripture, we have the 1. Old Testament (Law), 2. Gospels (fulfillment of the Law) and 3. New Testament (grace and truth), which begins with the Acts of the Apostles.

Many Pastors teach a mixture of tradition, legalism (law), and grace. Whenever you hear "You must do something" to be made right with God, you are hearing Law and not grace. Let's practice seeing and hearing the difference between Law and Grace so we can rightly divide Scripture and discern when we hear correct teaching.

EXAMPLES OF WRONG TEACHING (LAW)
Check those you've heard before.

1. Ask God for forgiveness daily so you can stay forgiven. ____
2. Penance (self-punishment or reporting sins to a Priest) is required to be made right with God. ____
3. You earn your sanctification. ____
4. A murderer can't go to heaven. ____
5. You shouldn't get a Tattoo. ____
6. You shouldn't spend time with non-Christians. ___
7. We have church rules that you need to know about. ____
8. Too much grace is a bad thing. ____
9. We need a balance of Law and Grace. ____
10. Fasting will make you right with God. ____

11. You can't go to heaven if you die with unconfessed sin. ____
12. God is not going to be happy with you about that. ____
13. I'm a moral person, so I'm going to heaven when I die. ____
14. I go to church every week, so I'm going to heaven. ____
15. That backslider is not a real Christian. ____
16. I made a deal with God. I'll do this if he'll do that. ____
17. What other "legal" statements have you heard before?

    ____

"Legalism" has also been described as a "Religious Spirit." In legalism, religious tradition or man-made rules take precedence over Scripture. Are you starting to identify the Law?

Let's drive this home.

You might be legalistic if you:

1. Lack true joy.
2. Have no real victory over sin.
3. Place a higher value on church customs than biblical principles (bondage to religious tradition or denominational history).
4. Find yourself judging people for not abiding by church rules.
5. Feel God is mad at you due to lack of performance.
6. Obsessively focused on outward standards of dress or behavior.
7. Believe you have a corner on truth to the exclusion of other Christians.
8. Are you unsure of your Salvation or think you can lose your salvation.
9. Are seeking God's approval by your performance.
10. Are seeking God's approval by following the law.

EXAMPLES OF RIGHT TEACHING (GRACE AND TRUTH)

1. I am saved by grace. (Ephesians 2:8) ____
2. I am fully justified by grace. (Titus 3:7) ____
3. I am forgiven of all sin past, present, and future. (Ephesians 1:7-8) ____
4. God is madly in love with me. John 3:16, Romans 5:8, Romans 8:38-39 ____
5. Great power comes from grace. (Acts 4:33) ____
6. Grace gives you sufficiency in all things. (2 Corinthians 9:8) ____
7. The Holy Spirit IS the Spirit of Grace. (Hebrews 10:29) ____
8. Grace empowers me to overcome sin. (Romans 6:14-15) ____
9. Grace gives me the ability to be humble. (James 4:6) ____
10. Grace helps me to forgive others (Hebrews 12:14-15) ____

After receiving salvation by grace through faith, some teachers/preachers begin to fear that "too much" of the Gospel of grace will lead people to sin. This unfounded notion is referred to as "greasy grace." The devil's advocate will argue the downfall of too much grace. God has lavished His grace on us! He is FULL of Grace and Truth **(John 1:14)**. There's no such thing as "too much grace." Grace will lead people away from a life of sin.

Acts 20:24 KJV "But none of these things move me, neither I count my life dear unto myself, so that I might finish my course with joy, and the ministry, which I have received from the Lord Jesus, to testify to the Gospel of the Grace of God."

God's grace is "unearned and unmerited favor." We no longer try to earn God's acceptance by keeping the Law or through our good works when we understand grace. Jesus took our punishment for not being able to keep the Law. He gave us eternal life, His righteousness, and holiness.

Now that you understand Law and Grace, you can see that the Law never brought about morality. It only convicted people of sin. People were prone to sin before grace came to earth in the person of Jesus. If you are walking in sin, you don't understand the fullness of grace. **(Romans 6:14).** Sin can't have dominion over someone living under grace. **(Romans 6:1-2)**. The Gospel of Grace IS the Gospel of Jesus Christ. (**Acts 20:24**). It isn't possible to interpret grace as an excuse to sin more. **(Romans 6:15)**.

Jesus fulfilled all the requirements to restore us to a right relationship with God. Jesus paid the price because he loves us. God of the Old Testament is no longer angry at humanity because Jesus redeemed us through his blood.

Colossians 1:19-22 NLT "For God in all his fullness was pleased to live in Christ, and through him God reconciled everything to himself. He made peace with everything in heaven and on earth by means of Christ's blood on the cross. This includes you, who were once far away from God. You were his enemies, separated from him by your evil thoughts and actions. Yet now he has reconciled you to himself through the death of Christ in his physical body. As a result, he has brought you into his presence, and you are holy and blameless as you stand before him without a single fault."

Galatians 3:11 NLT "No one who relies on the Law is justified before God because "the righteous will live by faith."

MEMORIZATION VERSE: GALATIANS 5:18 NRSV(CE)

____

____

____

____

PERSONAL REFLECTION:
HOW IS HOLY SPIRIT SPEAKING TO YOU THROUGH THESE SCRIPTURES?

ANSWER KEY: LESSON 2.1: LAW AND GRACE

Ephesians 2:8 NRSV(CE) "For by grace you have been saved through faith, and this is not your own doing; it is the gift of God not the result of works, so that no one may boast."

Titus 3:7 NRSV(CE) "Having been justified by his grace, we might become heirs according to the hope of eternal life."

Ephesians 1:7-8 NRSV(CE) "In him we have redemption through his blood, the forgiveness of our trespasses, according to the riches of his grace that he lavished on us."

John 3:16 NRSV(CE) "For God so loved the world that he gave his only Son, so that everyone who believes in him may not perish but may have eternal life."

Acts 4:33 NRSV(CE) "With great power the apostles gave their testimony to the resurrection of the Lord Jesus, and great grace was upon them all."

2 Corinthians 9:8 NAB(RE) "Moreover, God is able to make every grace abundant for you, so that in all things, always having all you need, you may have an abundance for every good work."

Zechariah 12:10 NRSV(CE) "Then I will pour out a spirit of grace."

Romans 6:14-15 NRSV(CE) "For sin will have no dominion over you, since you are not under Law but under grace. What then? Should we sin because we are not under law but under grease? By no means!"

James 4:6 NRSV(CE) "But he gives all the more grace; therefore, it says, "God opposes the proud, but gives grace to the humble."

Hebrews 12:14-15 NRSV(CE) "Pursue peace with everyone and holiness without which no one will see the Lord. See to it that no one fails to obtain the grace of God; that no root of bitterness

springs up and causes trouble, and through it, many become defiled."

John 1:14 NRSV(CE) "The Word became flesh and lived among us, and we have seen his glory, the glory as of a father's only son, full of grace and truth."

Romans 6:1-2 NRSV(CE) "What then are we to say? Should we continue in sin in order that grace may abound? By no means! How can we who died to sin go on living in it?"

Acts 20:24 NKJV "The ministry which I received from the Lord Jesus, to testify to the gospel of the grace of God."

Galatians 5:18 NRSV(CE) "If you are led by the Spirit, you are not under the Law."

LESSON 2.2

RIGHTEOUSNESS

Righteousness is the ability to stand in the presence of God as if we've never sinned. This is not according to what we've done, but what Jesus has done for us at the cross.

2 Corinthians 5:21 NRSV(CE)

____

____

____

____

We can't be made right with God through our works or good behavior, so God gave the gift of His Righteousness to those who believe in Jesus. Understanding your Righteousness in Jesus brings you into intimacy with God. Jesus offers us His Righteousness (right standing) before God as a gift so that we can stand in God's presence without shame, guilt, or condemnation.

Romans 5:17 NRSV(CE) "If because of the one man's (Adam's) trespass, death exercised dominion (over us) through that one,

much more surely will those who receive the abundance of grace and the gift of righteousness exercise dominion in life through the one man, Jesus Christ."

Grace and Righteousness are gifts to pull you out of a life of sin so you can reign in life with dominion and authority. This gift means that Jesus has put you in right standing with God, and God sees you as if you've never sinned. He took every one of your sins (past, present, and future) and nailed them to the cross. Now, you are restored to a right relationship with God and blessed by God with every spiritual blessing because of what Jesus has done for you.

Ephesians 1:3 NRSV(CE) "Blessed be the God and Father of our Lord Jesus Christ, who has blessed us in Christ with every spiri-tual blessing in the heavenly places."

You can never lose your Righteousness. Sin won't take it away. You didn't do anything to be righteous, so you can't do anything to become unrighteous. God imputes Jesus's Righteousness on you, not because of what you do, but because of what Jesus did for you. In God's eyes, you have become righteous, holy, sinless, and unblemished because when he sees you, he sees Jesus in you.

Romans 3:22-23 NIV

____

____

____

____

The Bible declares that Jesus Christ is the source of our Righteousness.

Romans 14:17 NRSV(CE) "For the kingdom of God is not food and drink but righteousness and peace and joy in the Holy Spirit."

God's Righteousness bestowed on believers is the foundation for right living in His power, not in ours. Righteousness is the foundation for

Godly character, conscience, and conduct. It is the basis for a hunger for God's word, forgiveness, hearing God's voice, and walking in the fruit of the Spirit. Righteousness is not you practicing "behavior modification" but allowing the Holy Spirit in you to do a "heart transformation."

2 Timothy 2:22 NRSV(CE) "Shun youthful passions and pursue righteousness, faith, love, and peace, along with those who call on the Lord from a pure heart."

1 Corinthians 6:11 NKJV "And such were some of you. But you were washed, you were sanctified, you were justified in the name of the Lord Jesus Christ and by the Spirit of our God."

You are made up of body, soul, and spirit. Your soul is your mind, will, and emotions. Your spirit is now a New Creation, and the Spirit of God that now lives in you. God's Righteousness has been deposited in you. Your purpose in life is to align your body and soul to line up with the Spirit of Grace and Righteousness. When body and soul line up with the Spirit, you receive healing, revelation, peace, joy, and the power of God to live out your new life.

1 Corinthians 1:30 NIV "It is because of him that you are in Christ Jesus, who has become for us wisdom from God that is, our righteousness, holiness and redemption."

Turn to God's Grace and embrace Righteousness, which is your compass, guiding you toward eternal life with God through Christ.

Romans 5:1 NRSV(CE) "Therefore, since we have been justified through faith, we have peace with God through our Lord Jesus Christ, through whom we have gained access by faith into this grace in which we now stand."

Jesus is the foundation for Righteousness and Righteousness is the foundation of Christianity.

1 Corinthians 3:11 NRSV(CE) "No one can lay any foundation other than the one already laid, which is Jesus Christ."

MEDITATE ON YOUR NEW RIGHTEOUSNESS

I am God's Righteousness. I am a son/daughter of the most high God. I walk in the peace, joy, and power of the Holy Spirit who lives in me. Sin no longer has any hold on me.

What you speak over yourself you grow up into. Speak life!

PERSONAL REFLECTION:
HOW IS HOLY SPIRIT SPEAKING TO YOU THROUGH THESE SCRIPTURES?

____

____

____

____

ANSWER KEY: LESSON 2.2: RIGHTEOUSNESS

2 Corinthians 5:21 NRSV(CE) "God made him (Jesus) who had no sin to be sin for us, so that in him we might become the righteousness of God."

Romans 3:22-23 NIV "Righteousness is given through faith in Jesus Christ to all who believe. There is no difference between Jew and Gentile, for all have sinned and fall short of the glory of God."

LESSON 3.1

REPENTANCE and RENEWING YOUR MIND

Repentance comes from the Greek word "Metanoia," meaning a "sincere change of mind and heart." That change causes you to renew your mind to "who you have become" in Christ and to move in that direction. Repentance brings about real change and is the fruit of God's grace working in our lives. It means to "change your mind" and to "turn back" to your new identity, which is the Righteousness of God.

In order to renew your mind you need to see yourself as God sees you. In His eyes you are made in His image, sinless, righteous sons and daughters and new creations. Right believing produces right living.

Acts 3:19 ESV "Repent therefore, and turn back, that your sins may be blotted out, that times of refreshing may come from the presence of the Lord."

Under the Old Testament (Law), you sin; then repent, then God blesses you. Under the New Testament (Grace), God has first blessed you with every spiritual blessing. When you sin, you repent because of what He has already done. It's not repentance that leads you to goodness; It's the goodness of God that leads you to repentance.

Romans 2:4 NIV "Do you show contempt for the riches of his kindness, forbearance, and patience, not realizing that God's kindness is intended to lead you to repentance?"

When you mess up, make a course correction and remind yourself that you are a living sacrifice. The Holy Spirit will never leave you. He is not there to condemn but to help you be transformed by the renewing of your mind.

Romans 12:1-2 ESV "Do not be conformed to this world, but be transformed by the renewal of your mind, that by testing you may discern what is the will of God, what is good and acceptable and perfect."

Living a victorious life starts with minor course corrections that deny the flesh when sin is presented and is accomplished by choosing Godly options. The more you do this, the easier it gets. It means taking each thought captive to the obedience of Christ.

2 Corinthians 10:5 NIV "We demolish arguments and every pretension that sets itself up against the knowledge of God, and we take captive every thought to make it obedient to Christ."

Ephesians 4:15 ESV

____

____

____

____

Repentance and renewing your mind are two sides of the same coin. Once you remember that sin is not what you want to do, you must replace those thoughts with something new.

Philippians 4:8 ESV "Finally, brothers, whatever is true, whatever is honorable, whatever is just, whatever is pure, whatever is lovely, whatever is commendable, if there is any excellence, if there is

anything worthy of praise, think about these things. What you have learned, received, heard, and seen in me, practice these things, and the God of peace will be with you."

Philippians 2:5 NKJV

____

____

____

____

The more you begin to capture sinful thoughts and replace them with what's worthy of praise, the more you will experience peace of mind, the love of God, and the fellowship of the Holy Spirit.

Romans 8:6 ESV "For to set the mind on the flesh is death, but to set the mind on the Spirit is life and peace."

Isaiah 26:3 ESV "You (Jesus) keep him in perfect peace whose mind is stayed on you (Jesus)."

How do you keep your mind on the Lord? It takes practice. Prayer, praise, worship, and meditating on Scripture are ways you renew your mind. When you practice these things His perfect peace comes up inside you.

No matter how bad things have been in the past or how distant you have felt from God, when you change your mind and turn back (repent), you will immediately encounter God's love and mercy waiting for you. The Lord will never leave you or forsake you. **(Deuteronomy 31:6).**

The power of Christ is at work in you to overcome past, present, and future difficulties and temptations. Salvation is a magnificent rescue that includes God's power to deliver us, make us whole, redeem us, and restore us to His original intent to live in holiness and purity.

Quit thinking the way you thought before you were born again. Start thinking about who you are growing in to. Begin to see yourself how God sees you. Look in the mirror and say the things God says about you.

ALL PARAPHRASED:

You are Wonderfully made (**Psalm 139:14**)

You are Honored and Precious in His sight (**Isaiah 43:4**)

You are God's special possession (**1 Peter 2:9**)

You are The light of the world (**Matthew 5:14**)

You are The apple of His eye (**Psalm 17:8**)

You are More than a conqueror (**Romans 8:37**)

You are God's temple (**1 Corinthians 3:16**)

You are God's favorite (**Psalm 30:7**)

You are dearly loved (**1 John 3:2**), (**1 John 4:16**)

You are Sons/Daughters of the Most High God (**Galatians 4:7**)

You are a New Creation (**2 Corinthians 5:17**)

You are Blessed (**Ephesians 1:3**)

You are Forgiven and Redeemed (**Ephesians 1:7**)

When you were born again, you turned from sin and death and were given the mind of the Holy Spirit and life.

John 14:26 CSB "But the Counselor, the Holy Spirit, whom the Father will send in my name, will teach you all things and remind you of everything I have told you."

Many people took the first step of Salvation (receiving forgiveness of sins) but never took the second step (renewing your mind). God did his part at the cross in Salvation. That is total Salvation of body, soul/mind, and spirit. There's a part God does and a part you do. If you want to grow closer to God and reduce the battle in your mind for carnal things, you must renew your mind.

Many sermons have been taught on what renewing your mind is and why it's essential. This book also teaches "how" to do it. Many people get saved and expect just to start thinking, acting, and doing things differently, but they "feel" the same. You look in the mirror and see the same person. Your thoughts are still your old thoughts. You didn't get a new brain. You have to capture each thought and change the way you think.

You have the mind of Christ in you, yet you still have your mind, which Scripture refers to as "free will." Renewing your mind is not trying to do better in your power. It's coming to know who you have become in Christ, and growing into your new identity,

Ephesians 4:18 (paraphrased) If you don't begin to think differently, then your understanding becomes clouded. You remain alienated from the life that God has intended for you.

Do you know the life God has planned for you is a better, richer, and more abundant life than you have planned for yourself? Knowing God's word is the first step to renewing your mind.

John 1:14 (paraphrased) says God's word became flesh in Jesus.

If you know God's word, then you know the mind of Christ. The Bible is inspired by the Holy Spirit, so as you read it He is activated to interpret it for you! Biblical meditation brings you in contact with God through Jesus. Pondering over a word by finding it everywhere it's used in the Bible (by concordance) or meditating on a verse or paragraph is a great way to renew your mind as you look for God's meaning behind the words. A fun meditation exercise is to see yourself in the story as you read Scripture. Try to see yourself as Jesus in Scripture. He has given you his authority and his name to use. In order to grow up into His likeness you begin to see yourself as Him. Disciples imitate the Master.

You will succeed in getting different results if you are willing to change your thoughts. Without renewing your mind, God will have no power in your life. Here's a statement that fits every one of us: "Our life is going in the direction of our dominant thoughts and words."

When you were born again, God gave YOU the power to change yourself and your situation. Your circumstances will change if you change how you think and what you say about yourself and the situation. Your thoughts and words are very powerful. Your life today is a direct result of what you spoke over yourself and prayed about 6 months ago.

Mark 4:1-20 is an essential scripture on how to renew your mind and get supernatural results in your relationships, health, finances, and walk with God. It starts with a seed, which is planted in the ground, which is your mind. Many of us have planted weeds and are expecting a fruit tree.

Consider that all life on this planet begins with a seed. Every plant, animal, and even every human began with a seed. We began with our fathers' seed. Jesus's life began with a seed that God planted in Mary. The seed produces fruit. The seed that starts in your mind is the seed that determines your future.

The parable in **Mark 4:3-7** talks about the seeds we plant in our minds. Is your mind a hardened path? That's called religion. In a mind with a hardened path, things have to be done a certain way. There is no room for the Holy Ghost to operate.

A mind with stoney ground starts out strong but as soon as things get difficult we quit. The roots don't go deep. Faith and understanding is surface level. Stones are anything that holds people back due to old hurts, pain, pride, physical or mental abuse, and limits a person by their past. The Holy Spirit will clean the stones out when we let Him so we can be productive in the Kingdom.

Thorns and thistles are bad habits and an emphasis on the cares of this world that choke the Spirit. "I like to play video games." "I'm on TikTok for hours." "I have 15 mins for morning devotions," and then our day is full of the cares of this world. Seeds that the Holy Ghost has for us this day to walk in power and abundance are choked out because the day is full of thorns and thistles.

By renewing your mind your ability to operate in good soil is multiplied, producing 30, 60, and 100 fold. **(Mark 4:8)**. You can measure your soil by how much time you spend with God each day. How often do you call on him to provide the answer? Not just during the time you set aside for devotions, but do you ask God, hear from God (through the Holy Spirit), and walk with God all day? You are not just walking with God as Adam and Eve did. You are walking AS GOD because with a renewed mind, you ARE JESUS to the World, and you walk with His power to do good, heal the sick, and raise the dead because the Holy Spirit is in you.

It may take time to "grow up into the likeness of Christ." **(2 Corinthians 3:18)**. It takes remembering your new identity and renewing your mind to replace bad habits with good habits. You can't just stop doing something wrong. You have to start doing something good. In order to renew your mind you have to fill the empty void with the leading of Holy Spirit in that area.

1 Peter 1:23 (paraphrased) says God's word is an incorruptible seed. When you read it, hear it, and plant it in your mind, it grows roots down to your heart and produces harvestable fruit.

There is seedtime and harvest time. Renewing your mind is the seedtime. Know what Scripture you are standing on (this is covered in Chapter 6.1 on prayer) then practice brings the harvest. You are not left without Spiritual tools to help in all these things.

Ephesians 6:11-13 NKJV "Put on the whole armor of God, that you may be able to stand against the wiles of the devil. For we do not wrestle against flesh and blood, but against principalities,

against powers, against the rulers of the darkness of this age, against spiritual hosts of wickedness in the heavenly places. Therefore take up the whole armor of God, that you may be able to withstand in the evil day, and having done all, to stand."

Ephesians 6:15-17 NKJV "Stand therefore, having girded your waist with truth, having put on the breastplate of Righteousness, and having shod your feet with the preparation of the Gospel of peace; above all, taking the shield of faith with which you will be able to quench all the fiery darts of the wicked one. And take the helmet of Salvation and the sword of the Spirit, which is the word of God."

Satan has no hold on you, and now you must learn to stand on biblical truths. Put on the armor of God, and take every thought captive to the obedience of Christ so you can learn to renew your mind and stand against the lies and temptations of the devil.

MEMORIZATION VERSE

2 Corinthians 10:5 NKJV "Bring every thought into captivity to the obedience of Christ."

PERSONAL REFLECTION:
HOW IS HOLY SPIRIT SPEAKING TO YOU THROUGH THESE SCRIPTURES?

____

____

____

____

ANSWER KEY LESSON 3.1: REPENTANCE AND RENEWING YOUR MIND

Ephesians 4:15 ESV "Speaking the truth in love, we are to grow up in every way into him who is the head, into Christ."

Philippians 2:5 NKJV "Let this mind be in you which was also in Christ Jesus."

Mark 4:1-20 ESV

"1 He began to teach beside the sea, and a very large crowd gath-ered about him, so that he got into a boat and sat in it on the sea, and the whole crowd was beside the sea on the land.

2 And he was teaching them many things in parables, and in his teaching he said to them:

3 "Listen! Behold, a sower went out to sow.

4 And as he sowed, some seed fell along the path, and the birds came and devoured it.

5 Other seed fell on rocky ground, where it did not have much soil, and immediately it sprang up, since it had no depth of soil.

6 And when the sun rose, it was scorched, and since it had no root, it withered away.

7 Other seed fell among thorns, and the thorns grew up and choked it, and it yielded no grain.

8 And other seeds fell into good soil and produced grain, growing up and increasing and yielding thirtyfold and sixtyfold and a hundredfold."

9 And he said, "He who has ears to hear, let him hear."

10 And when he was alone, those around him with the twelve asked him about the parables.

11 And he said to them, "To you has been given the secret of the kingdom of God, but for those outside everything is in parables,

12 so that they may indeed see but not perceive, and may indeed hear but not understand, lest they should turn and be forgiven."

13 And he said to them, "Do you not understand this parable? How then will you understand all the parables?"

14 "The sower sows the word.

15 And these are the ones along the path, where the word is sown: when they hear, Satan immediately comes and takes away the word that is sown in them.

16 And these are the ones sown on rocky ground: the ones who, when they hear the word, immediately receive it with joy.

17 And they have no root in themselves, but endure for a while; then, when tribulation or persecution arises on account of the word, immediately they fall away.

18 And others are the ones sown among thorns. They are those who hear the word,

19 but the cares of the world and the deceitfulness of riches and the desires for other things enter in and choke the word, and it proves unfruitful.

20 But those that were sown on the good soil are the ones who hear the word and accept it and bear fruit, thirtyfold and sixtyfold and a hundredfold."

Deuteronomy 31:6 ESV "Be strong and courageous. Do not fear or be in dread of them, for it is the Lord your God who goes with you. He will not leave you or forsake you."

2 Corinthians 3:18 ESV "We all, with unveiled face, beholding the glory of the Lord, are being transformed into the same image from

one degree of glory to another. For this comes from the Lord who is the Spirit."

LESSON 3:2

WATER BAPTISM

I was baptized in the Catholic Church before my first birthday. I was baptized again when I joined the Baptist church (believers baptism). On two separate occasions, I visited the Holy Land and both times, I was baptized in the Jordan River.

I searched the Scriptures to see what was "legally required" regarding Baptism. I referred to this in the preface when I said I wish I had been taught some things earlier. Looking for legal requirements puts us back under the Law. Baptism, like accepting Jesus as Lord and Savior, is a heart issue, not a head issue. Do you love Jesus and want to follow him? Then why wouldn't you want to be born again and baptized?

Is water baptism required to go to heaven? Not at all. In **Matthew 27:38** two thieves were crucified with Jesus at the cross. One thief says "I believe." To that one, Jesus says, "You will be with me in paradise." (**Luke 23:43**). He was not baptized with water, but Jesus says he will go to heaven based on faith in Him.

Just a note to my Catholic friends: Jesus did not send this thief to Purgatory (a holding place to work off your sins) before he was welcomed into heaven. If we could work off our sins, then Jesus died for no reason. Jesus took care of all our sins at the cross. Jesus says to the sinner; **"You believe in me, so TODAY you will be with me in heaven/paradise." (Luke 23:43).** There is no sacrifice we can offer and nothing we can do to work off our sins. The idea that we can work off our sins is an example of legalism and a misunderstanding of grace for what Jesus did for us at the cross.

The Holy Spirit makes his home in you as soon as you accept Jesus as Lord and Savior. This is the "First Baptism." **(Galatians 3:27).**

So why do we need a "Second Baptism" with water? Jesus gave us two Holy ordinances (orders). Communion/Eucharist (breaking of bread) and Water Baptism. Both are Holy remembrances that identify us with Christ and the new covenant he made in his blood. **(Luke 22:19-20)**

Water Baptism is an outward sign of an inward decision. Did Jesus need to be baptized to go to heaven? No, Jesus did this as an example to us. Do you want to follow Jesus? Then be baptized!

What type of water is required at Baptism? Alarm bells should be going off in your head right now! The fact that religious leaders are even concerned about the "type" of water should tell you this is religion under the Law and not the New Testament Gospel of Grace. Here are the preferred "rules" of Baptism by many religious leaders and denominations. Immersion in "moving water" is the first choice. That is a river, ocean, lake, or other outdoor water in its natural environment. Due to its proximity and convenience religious leaders have moved water baptism to indoor pools, troughs, and tubs.

In some cases, religious leaders think the water must be "blessed first." Some immerse, pour or sprinkle the water on the person being baptized. (Preference in that order.) The amount and form of water are not essential to God. These preferences do not make Baptism more or less effective. If you are in the desert and there is no water around, I suppose someone could spit on you if you feel the need to be baptized with water at that moment. Spit can be Holy. **(Mark 8:23)**

I was at dinner in Vermont when the man I was with finally understood Baptism. He wanted to be baptized right then! After dinner, we went outside and found it was snowing. I picked up a handful of snow and touched it on his forehead, abdomen, and across his heart in the sign of the cross. I baptized him with "frozen water" (snow) in the name of the Father, Son, and Holy Spirit. Legal religious circles might think it invalid, but God was pleased.

Baptism is a beautiful demonstration to the outside World of what you have already decided. Only denominational religious laws and rules specify the type and amount of water. God does not have such requirements.

Water does not wash away our sins; the blood of Jesus does. Baptism does not save or secure us; accepting Jesus as Lord and Savior does that. Water baptism represents a believer's identification with dying to self, being buried with Christ and in his resurrection, being raised to walk a brand new life.

Romans 6:3-4 ESV "Do you not know that all of us who have been baptized into Christ Jesus were baptized into his death? We were buried therefore with him by baptism into death, in order that, just as Christ was raised from the dead by the glory of the Father, we too might walk in newness of life."

Re-baptism is unnecessary, or we would need to be re-baptized after every sin. Can you be re-baptized? That's up to you and your Pastor. If you have a new understanding of Baptism and want to be baptized again with a new heart and appreciation, you may do so, but it has no bearing on your eternal salvation.

In the Great Commission, Jesus commanded His disciples (including us) to make disciples and baptize them.

Matthew 28:19 ESV

____

____

____

____

As people heard Philip's message, they were baptized.

Acts 8:12 ESV "When they believed Philip as he preached good news about the kingdom of God and the name of Jesus Christ, they were baptized, both men and women."

Acts 2:41 NIV "Those who accepted his message were baptized, and about three thousand were added to their number that day."

Acts 2:38 ESV "Peter said to them, "Repent and be baptized every one of you in the name of Jesus Christ for the forgiveness of your sins, and you will receive the gift of the Holy Spirit."

When you are baptized into Him, you die with him and are resurrected with him through faith. Jesus took on all the sins of the World at the cross. He took all your sins. So when you die with Him your sins are gone. A dead person can not sin! When you are in Him you also are resurrected with Him into new life. You are a new creature with a new start and a new incorruptible seed in you with the new power of Holy Spirit to walk like Jesus.

1 Peter 1:23 NKJV "Being born again, not of corruptible seed, but of incorruptible, by the word of God, which liveth and abideth forever."

Colossians 2:12 ESV "Having been buried with him in Baptism, in which you were also raised with him through faith."

In every depiction of Baptism in the Bible, we witness the symbolic act of leaving behind the old life and embracing a new one. Through Baptism, we openly acknowledge the transformative power of Jesus's death and resurrection by obeying his command to be baptized. We align ourselves with the profound significance of the cross and resurrection, experiencing liberation from the dominion of sin.

MEDITATION VERSE: ACTS 22:16 ESV

PERSONAL REFLECTION:
HOW IS HOLY SPIRIT SPEAKING TO YOU THROUGH THESE SCRIPTURES?

ANSWER KEY LESSON 3:2: WATER BAPTISM

Matthew 27:38 ESV "Then two robbers were crucified with him, one on the right and one on the left."

Galatians 3:27 ESV "For as many of you as were baptized into Christ have put on Christ."

Luke 22:19-20 ESV "This is my body, which is given for you. Do this in remembrance of me." And likewise the cup after they had eaten, saying, "This cup that is poured out for you is the new covenant in my blood."

Mark 8:23 ESV "He took the blind man by the hand and led him out of the village, and when he had spit on his eyes and laid his hands on him, he asked him, "Do you see anything?"

Matthew 28:19 ESV "Go therefore and make disciples of all nations, baptizing them in the name of the Father and of the Son and the Holy Spirit."

Acts 22:16 ESV "Now why do you wait? Rise and be baptized and wash away your sins, calling on his name."

LESSON 4.1

INTRO TO THE HOLY SPIRIT

The Holy Spirit, being the Spirit of God, is indeed God Himself. Before the resurrection of Jesus, the Holy Spirit was bestowed upon only a few individuals at a time. Some were known as the prophets of old. At the beginning of the Old Testament we witness the presence of Holy Spirit during the act of creation as the **"Spirit of God hovered over the deep." (Genesis 1:2 CSB)**. Each time the Holy Spirit moves, He points people to God the Father through Jesus. This truth is held in the Old Testament and remains unchanged through the present day.

Before Jesus ascended to heaven, He told His disciples to return to Jerusalem and wait. They were about to receive an amazing gift: the Baptism of the Holy Spirit. Ever since this time (called Pentecost) the Holy Spirit has been poured out on all believers that are born again.

Acts 1:4-5 CSB "While he was with them, he commanded them not to leave Jerusalem, but to wait for the Father's promise. "Which," he said, "you have heard me speak about; John baptized with water, but you will be baptized with the Holy Spirit in a few days."

The Holy Spirit is also known as the Holy Ghost, the Spirit of Truth, the Spirit of Grace, Wisdom, the Anointing, etc. He presents Himself as fire, wind, water, mist, breath, conscience, a still small voice, and limitless other manifestations.

The Holy Spirit is a person who has feelings. You can trust Him to guide you through life. The Holy Spirit will never leave nor forsake you, even if you sin or miss the mark. He is the One that can put you back on course. You received the fullness of the Holy Spirit with all his power when you were born again. Nothing was left out. It's like being given a rocket ship that you must learn how to operate in. Let's look at the friend, counselor, and direct access to God you've been given.

You have an understanding of water baptism. Next comes the Holy Spirit, who baptizes with fire!

Matthew 3:11 CSB (John the Baptist speaking) "I baptize you with water for repentance, but the one who is coming after me is more powerful than I. I am not worthy to remove his sandals. He will baptize you with the Holy Spirit and fire."

Have you heard the expression "Baptism by Fire?" Many worldly expressions originated in Scripture. In this case, the Holy Spirit brings peace and joy to the believer through Holy Spirit fire, which consumes one's old self-centered life and leads one to a purified life in the Spirit.

Hebrews 12:29 CSB "Our God is a consuming fire."

The Holy Spirit is the fullness of God that lives in you.

1 Corinthians 3:16 CSB "Don't you yourselves know that you are God's temple and that the Spirit of God lives in you?"

For further study on the Holy Spirit see **Romans 8:1-17.**

In Chapter 6.2 of this book, you'll learn how to release the power of the Holy Spirit (who raised Jesus from the dead and lives in you) through prayer. The Holy Spirit will teach you how to walk in power like Jesus. Glory be to God!

Colossians 2:10 CSB "You have been filled by him, who is the head over every ruler and authority."

Mark 16:17 CSB

____

____

____

____

1 Corinthians 6:19-20 CSB "Don't you know that your body is the temple of the Holy Spirit who is in you, whom you have from God? You are not your own, for you were bought at a price. So, glorify God with your body."

Living the Christian life without the power of the Holy Spirit is unattainable. The moment we are born-again, the Holy Spirit equips us with everything necessary to walk like Jesus and represent Him in our daily lives.

2 Peter 1:3 CSB "His divine power has given us EVERYTHING required for life and godliness through the knowledge of Him who called us by his glory and goodness."

Romans 8:14 NLT "For all who are led by the Spirit of God are children of God."

Every Christian who is saved should have a desire to identify what their spiritual gifts are. Why is it essential for you to identify your spiritual gifts? So that you can live the life God intended for you, which is to love and serve God and the people around you.

Ephesians 4:12-13 CSB "Gifts were given to equip the saints for the work of ministry, to build up the body of Christ, until we all reach unity in the faith and in the knowledge of God's Son, growing into maturity with a stature measured by Christ's fullness."

Below is a list of gifts given by the Holy Spirit:

SUPERNATURAL GIFTS

Words of Wisdom **1 Corinthians 12:8** (Revelation gift)

Words of Knowledge **1 Corinthians 12:8** (Revelation gift)

Distinguishing of Spirits **1 Corinthians 12:10** (Revelation gift)

Gift of Faith **1 Corinthians 12:9** (Power gift)

Gift of Healing **1 Corinthians 12:9**, **1 Corinthians 12:28** (Power gift)

Gift of Miracles **1 Corinthians 12:10, 1 Corinthians 12:28** (Power gift)

Prophecy (**1 Corinthians 12:10, Romans 12:6** (Verbal gift)

Various kinds of tongues **1 Corinthians 12:10, 1 Cor 12:28** (Verbal gift)

Interpretation of tongues **1 Corinthians 12:10** (Verbal gift)

HELP GIFTS

Gift of Helps (**1 Corinthians 12:28**)

Gift of Administration (**1 Corinthians 12:28**)

Gift of Service/Serving (**Romans 12:7**)

Gift of Exhortation (**Romans 12:8**)

Gift of Mercy (**Romans 12:8**)

Gift of Giving (**Romans 12:8**)

Gift of Leadership (**Romans 12:8**)

Gift of Teaching (**Romans 12: 7, 1 Corinthians 12:28, Ephesians 4:11**)

Gift of Apostleship (**1 Corinthians 12:28, Ephesians 4:11**)

Gift of Prophet (**1 Corinthians 12:28, Ephesians 4:11**)

Gift of Evangelist (**Ephesians 4:11**)

Gift of Pastor (**Ephesians 4:11**)

The "gifts of the Spirit" (supernatural and help gifts) and the "fruit of the Spirit" (love, joy, peace, patience, etc.) display God's character. As His representatives on earth, we need to develop both. The gifts and the fruit of the Spirit were given for the common good so that each of us can help build up the body of Christ.

Galatians 5:22-23 CSB "The fruit of the Spirit is love, joy, peace, patience, kindness, goodness, faithfulness, gentleness, and self-control. The Law is not against such things."

Fruitfulness holds significant weight in the Bible. You can measure your walk with the Holy Spirit by the manifestation of the fruit of the Spirit he has given you. Do you see evidence of the fruit of the Spirit in your life? **(Galatians 5:22-23 above)**.

Which ones do you have?

____

____

____

____

Which ones would you like to develop?

____

____

____

____

John 15:8 CSB "My Father is glorified by this: that you produce much fruit and prove to be my disciples."

God says all 21 Spiritual gifts above are worthless if you don't operate them in love. Why? Because you won't need any of those gifts in heaven. The only gift you will carry with you to heaven is love. It would be wise to practice the love of God and others on earth to prepare for eternity. Love God and Love others is your service to God. The 21 gifts above are for your service to others.

1 Corinthians 13:1-3 CSB "If I speak human or angelic tongues but do not have love, I am a noisy gong or a clanging cymbal. If I have the gift of prophecy and understand all mysteries and all knowledge, and if I have all faith so that I can move mountains but do not have love, I am nothing. And if I give away all my possessions, and if I give over my body in order to boast but do not have love, I gain nothing."

Ephesians 4:11-12 CSB "He gave some to be apostles, some prophets, some evangelists, some pastors, and teachers, to equip the saints for the work of ministry, to build up the body of Christ."

God wants to equip you with as many gifts of the Spirit as you desire. Jesus moved in all of them. We may have a predisposition to one or more of the gifts but we can choose any or all of them to develop with the help of the Holy Spirit. When he came to live in us, he brought ALL THE GIFTS. He left nothing out.

As we practice the gifts, we become more proficient in using them and see more results. Those who practice one gift over another have been said to have a "special anointing." The truth is that there are no "special anointings" or "mantles"; they are just people who have practiced one gift more than another.

Peter explains what it means to be a Christian living for God.

1 Peter 4:10-11 NIV "Each of you should use whatever gift you have received to serve others, as faithful stewards of God's grace in

its various forms. If anyone speaks, they should do so as one who speaks the very words of God. If anyone serves, they should do so with the strength God provides, so that in all things God may be praised through Jesus Christ."

1 Corinthians 3:13 CSB

____

____

____

____

Jesus commands all believers to evangelize, make disciples, heal the sick, and preach the kingdom of God. He gives us supernatural gifts of the Holy Spirit to carry out these instructions. Many Christians are happy to read their Bibles and go to church but never put what they've learned into action. Unfortunately, many churches only teach a few of the gifts and don't offer a platform to exercise all the gifts of the Spirit. Even worse, some churches teach that the gifts of the Spirit were only given to the original disciples and ceased to exist today. Let it be known that the gifts of the Spirit are all available and in manifestation for those who will practice them. Jesus has given us direction in Scripture, so no other word from God is required before we become doers of the word.

James 1:22 CSB "Be doers of the word and not hearers only, deceiving yourselves."

PERSONAL REFLECTION:
HOW IS HOLY SPIRIT SPEAKING TO YOU THROUGH THESE SCRIPTURES?

____

____

____

____

ANSWER KEY LESSON 4.1: INTRODUCTION TO THE HOLY SPIRIT

Mark 16:17 CSB "These signs will accompany those who believe: In my name, they will drive out demons; they will speak in new tongues."

1 Corinthians 12:7-11 CSB "A manifestation of the Spirit is given to each persona for the common good: to one is given a message of wisdom through the Spirit, to another, a message of knowledge by the same Spirit, to another, faith by the same Spirit, to nother, gifts of healing by the one Spirit, to another, the performing of miracles, to another, prophecy, to another, distinguishing between spirits, to another, different kinds of tongues, to another, interpretation of tongues. One and the same Spirit is active in all these, distributing to each person as he wills."

1 Corinthians 12:28 CSB "God has appointed these in the church: first apostles, second prophets, third teachers, next miracles, then gifts of healing, helping, leading, various kinds of tongues."

Romans 12:6-8 CSB "According to the grace given to us, we have different gifts: If prophecy, use it according to the proportion of one's faith; if service, use it in service; if teaching, in teaching; if exhorting, in exhortation; giving, with generosity; leading, with diligence; showing mercy, with cheerfulness."

Ephesians 4:11 CSB "He himself gave some to be apostles, some prophets, some evangelists, some pastors and teachers."

1 Corinthians 13:13 CSB "Now these three remain: faith, hope, and love; but the greatest of these is love."

LESSON 4.2

THE BAPTISM OF THE HOLY SPIRIT

The "Baptism of the Holy Spirit" has different meanings in different denominations. For purposes of introduction, we will stick with what is known in Scripture. By rightly dividing Scripture, we see John the Baptist (in the Gospels) at the Jordan River doing water baptisms.

Matthew 3:11 CSB "I baptize you with water for repentance. But after me comes one who is more powerful than I, whose sandals I am not worthy to carry. He will baptize you with the Holy Spirit and fire."

In the Gospels, Jesus speaks of a future "Baptism of the Holy Spirit" that will take place as part of the New Covenant in the New Testament. After Jesus's death and resurrection, he says to wait in Jerusalem for the "Baptism of the Holy Spirit."

Acts 1:8 CSB

____

____

____

____

Acts 2:1-6 CSB "When the day of Pentecost had come, they were all together in one place. And suddenly there came from heaven a noise like a violent rushing wind, and it filled the whole house where they were sitting. And there appeared to them tongues as of fire distributing themselves, and they rested on each one of them. And they were all filled with the Holy Spirit and began to speak with other tongues, as the Spirit was giving them utterance."

The disciples were filled with the Holy Spirit, which activated all the gifts. At Pentecost they were exercising one of the gifts: speaking in tongues.

Acts 19:6 CSB

____

____

____

____

The water baptism in the Gospels was for repentance and closed out the old covenant. In chapter 3.2 we learned that water baptism today is an outward sign of an inward decision to follow Jesus and in chapter 3.1 that repentance is simply changing your mind to who you already are as a new creation in Christ.

From Pentecost through today, anyone who became a born-again believer was immediately baptized with the fullness of the Holy Spirit and received all His gifts. No further baptism is found in Scripture that activates the gifts of the Spirit.

It's fair to say that some Christians don't desire all the gifts of the Holy Spirit. For example, not all Christians begin to speak in tongues when they receive the baptism of the Holy Spirit. However, all the gifts of the Spirit have all been deposited in your bank account. You choose when to draw them out.

Gifts of the Spirit are given to unify the church and give power and boldness to witness to unbelievers. Spending a little extra time on tongues in this book seems necessary because of all the gifts; it is least understood and can cause the most division.

Some Preachers/Teachers use the term "Baptism of the Holy Spirit" to exclusively designate the activation of the gift of "Speaking in tongues." Scripture describes more than one kind of tongue. Speaking or praying in unknown tongues is for your edification.

1 Corinthians 14:2-4 CSB "He who speaks in a tongue does not speak to men but to God. Indeed, no one understands him; he utters mysteries in the Spirit. but he who prophesies speaks to men for their edification, encouragement, and comfort. The one who speaks in a tongue edifies himself, but the one who prophesies edifies the church."

1 Corinthians 14:14 CSB "For if I pray in a tongue, my spirit prays, but my understanding is unfruitful."

You might also receive a gift of tongues unknown to you but known to others.

Acts 2:6-11 CSB "When this sound occurred, a crowd came together and was confused because each one heard them speaking in his language. They were astounded, saying, "Look, aren't all these who are speaking Galileans? How is it that each of us can hear them in our native language? Parthians, Medes, Elamites; those who live in Mesopotamia, Judea and Cappadocia, Pontus and Asia, Phrygia and Pamphylia, Egypt and the parts of Libya near Cyrene; visitors from Rome (both Jews and converts), Cretans and Arabs - we hear them declaring the magnificent acts of God in our own tongues."

Praying in tongues is the gift of the Holy Spirit praying for you and through you. If you choose this gift, God will be praying for you in an unknown language. He will pray for things you need that you don't even know you need. When you pray in tongues, you are praying in a language that Satan can not understand. Satan can not interfere with a prayer he can not understand.

Romans 8:26-27 CSB "In the same way the Spirit also helps us in our weakness, because we do not know what to pray for as we should, but the Spirit himself intercedes for us with inexpressible groanings. And he who searches our hearts knows the mind of the Spirit because he intercedes for the saints according to the will of God."

To pray in tongues, you open your mouth and move your vocal cords. The Holy Spirit does not take over your vocal cords. You make the sound and he will use the sound to pray through you. Do not speak known words or syllables. It may start as one syllable only (like a baby learning to speak). As with any gift, you must practice this to increase your vocabulary.

It is helpful to pray this way when you don't know how to pray or what to pray for, or when your human senses overcome your faith.

There are at least three types of tongues. 1. The personal prayer tongue that edifies you does not require interpretation. **(1 Corinthians 14:2).** 2. The prophetic tongue that edifies the church requires interpretation. **(1 Corinthians 14:27).** 3. The proof tongue is an actual foreign language that you have never learned but are supernaturally able to speak. **(Acts 2:9-11).**

Here are three simple exercises to improve hearing of the voice of the Holy Spirit.

1. Read the New Testament. The more familiar you become with the Word, the more familiar you will become with the Holy

Spirit. Know that he is already speaking to you. It's just a matter of recognizing his voice.
2. Remove distractions. Set aside a time daily for prayer and worship. The more you learn to quiet your mind, the easier it becomes to hear His voice.
3. Practice the first steps so you can be trusted with the next instructions for your life. Why would God give you more opportunities to partner with the Holy Spirit if you haven't spent the time to get to know Him?

Do steps 1 and 2 if you want to hear the Holy Spirit better. The will of God is revealed progressively. God is waiting for you to obey what He has already spoken.

The Holy Spirit will give you the time and desire to read the Word, pray, and worship. It is up to you to be consistent in the things He desires for you. Many Christians want God to show up or to have a supernatural encounter that will instill a new daily devotion to the word of God, Still it's up to you to have discipline in your daily decisions despite your emotions, preferences, and distractions of day-to-day life.

MEDITATION VERSE

1 John 2:6 CSB "The one who says he abides in Him (Jesus) ought himself to walk in the same manner as He (Jesus) walked."

You know you are walking with the Holy Spirit when:

1. You have an increased love of God's word. **Romans 8:5**
2. Sin and things of the world will lose their appeal. **Galatians 5:16**
3. You stay in peace even when pressure mounts. **Galatians 5:16**
4. You walk in the fruits of the Spirit. **Galatians 5:22**
5. You walk in the gifts and supernatural power of the Spirit. **Acts 1:8**

6. You demonstrate the love of Jesus in words, deeds and actions. **Colossians 3:12**

PERSONAL REFLECTION:
HOW IS HOLY SPIRIT SPEAKING TO YOU THROUGH THESE SCRIPTURES?

___

___

___

___

ANSWER KEY LESSON 4.2: SPIRITUAL GIFTS

Acts 1:8 CSB "You will receive power when the Holy Spirit has come on you, and you will be my witnesses in Jerusalem, in all Judea and Samaria, and to the ends of the earth."

Acts 19:6 CSB "When Paul had laid his hands upon them, the Holy Spirit came on them, and they began speaking with tongues and prophesying."

1 Corinthians 14:2 CSB "For the person who speaks in a tongue is not speaking to people but to God, since no one understands him; he speaks mysteries in the Spirit."

1 Corinthians 14:27 CSB "If anyone speaks in a tongue, there are to be only two, or at the most three, each in turn, and let someone interpret."

Romans 8:5 CSB "For those who live according to the flesh have their minds set on the things of the flesh, but those who live according to the Spirit have their minds set on the things of the Spirit."

Galatians 5:16 CSB " I say, then, walk by the Spirit and you will certainly not carry out the desire of the flesh."

Colossians 3:12 CSB "As God's chosen ones, holy and dearly loved, put on compassion, kindness, humility, gentleness, and patience, bearing with one another and forgiving one another if anyone has a grievance against another. Just as the Lord has forgiven you, so you are also to forgive."

LESSON 5.1

THE BIBLE: GOD'S WORD PT1

In this chapter you'll be introduced to some scriptural verses that illuminate the heart of God for the new believer. It will lead you to discover truths and values in Scripture for yourself. Hopefully, this sparks interest in the new believer towards further study as context and Scripture speaks for itself.

Many Christians know "about" God but do not "know God." The best way to get to know God is to spend time with him. Not just praying for what you need, but also in silence to hear his plans for you. At least 50% of good communication skills are "listening." Reading the Bible (especially the New Testament) is a great way to get to know God. When you know His Word, you know Him. The Holy Spirit in you is activated when you read Scripture because He inspired their writings. The Holy Spirit provides the interpretation for the revelation he provided through the writers.

The "Christian Old Testament" is the same as the current "Jewish/Hebrew Bible." The only difference is some of the order, and some books are combined in the modern-day Hebrew Bible.

Which books of the Bible begin and end the Old Testament?

The Gospels are the teachings of Jesus when he walked the earth. In the Gospels, Jesus fulfilled over 300 prophecies of the Old Testament pointing to and identifying himself as Messiah/the Christ.

Which books of the Bible are the Gospels?

When Jesus says, **"It is finished" (John 19:30)**, the prophecies of the Old Testament are fulfilled. Judgment for sin under the law was abolished, and the New Testament/New Covenant under grace was established. He also "finished" everything God sent Him to do, including defeating "sin and death" at the cross, taking all our infirmities, and opening direct access to heaven and God through the Holy Spirit for those who believe. Satan's rule and reign on earth was abolished and Jesus returned all authority on earth to those that follow Him.

Isaiah 53:4-5 NRSV "Surely he has borne our infirmities and carried our diseases; yet we accounted him stricken, struck down by God, and afflicted. But he was wounded for our transgressions, crushed for our iniquities; upon him was the punishment that made us whole, and by his bruises, we are healed."

John 16:7 HCSB "Nevertheless, I am telling you the truth. It is for your benefit that I go away, because if I don't go away the Counselor will not come to you. If I go, I will send him to you."

The Gospels close out the Old Testament and point to the New Testament. It is important to rightly divide Scripture so you are not brought back under the law. The New Covenant starts with the shed blood of Jesus, the resurrection and the introduction of the Holy Spirit, which begins in Acts.

Which books of the Bible encompass the New Testament/Covenant?

____

If you were to buy a "New Testament" Bible it would begin with the Gospels, but this is no different than a book titled "How to Give Birth" that starts with a chapter on "How to get pregnant."

You've been introduced to several names for "Holy Spirit." There are over a dozen names for God and over 100 references to God by His attributes. You should not be surprised to hear Christians refer to Holy Spirit, Jesus, or God by any number of names found in the Bible.

SOME NAMES OF GOD...

I AM: "God" (Exodus)

Adonai: "Lord/God" (Genesis)

El Shaddai: "God Almighty" (Genesis)

Elohim: "God/Creator, Mighty and Strong" (Genesis)

YHWH / YAHWEH: "Lord/God" (Exodus)

JEHOVAH: "Lord/God" (Exodus)

and many more…

SOME NAMES OF JESUS...

Yeshua (Hebrew name)

Emmanuel/Immanuel (Matthew)

Lamb of God (John)

Bread of Life (John)

Alpha and Omega (Revelation)

Messiah (Daniel)

Good Shepherd (John)

The Word (John)

Savior (John)

Son of Man (Matthew)

Son of God (Matthew)

and many more…

Even though Christians refer to the sixty-six books of the Bible as "books", many are not books at all. They are a compilation of writings, letters, poems, songs, prophesies, history and revelation. The complete Bible was written over 1500 years by about 40 authors. It is important to understand the context of the writing when applying scripture.

Context is the setting it was written in, the literary style (song, poem, history, prophesy, parable, etc), and to whom it was written. Sometimes taking a verse out of context will change its meaning. You can often read the verse before and after to understand its scriptural context.

The Old Testament was written in Hebrew and some Aramaic. Jesus' native language was likely a Galatian dialect of Jewish Aramaic. He also spoke Hebrew and was likely familiar with Greek since much of the area of his ministry was dominated by Greek culture. The New Testament was written in Greek. All the books of the Bible (Old and New Testaments) point to Jesus and reveal Jesus through the Holy Spirit's divinely inspired writings. The Holy Spirit wrote the entire Bible in cooperation with people. The Holy Spirit was present as each book of the Bible's Old and New Testaments were written. When you read Scripture, you are reading from the Word of God that lives in you. He is the underlying writer and interpreter of all Scripture.

2 Timothy 3:16 HCSB

____

____

____

____

God has chosen to reveal himself to humanity through general revelation and special revelation. General revelation refers to general truths that can be known about God through intelligent design in nature and the universe. Unbelievers can see the unmistakable hand of God in this way. Special revelation refers to specific truths that can be known about God through the supernatural. This includes physical appearances of God, dreams, visions, and the Word of God in Bible form and, most importantly, in the person of Jesus Christ.

Psalms 19:1 HCSB "The heavens declare the glory of God, and the sky proclaims the work of His hands."

Romans 1:20 HCSB "For His invisible attributes, that is, His eternal power and divine nature, have been seen since the creation of the world, being understood through what He has made. As a result, people are without excuse."

Romans 2:15 NLT

____

____

____

____

God has made peace with humanity through the blood of Jesus Christ. All judgment and justice are in the hands of Jesus who loves you through every circumstance and came to redeem us from the curse of the law.

Galatians 3:13-14 HCSB "Christ has redeemed us from the curse of the law by becoming a curse for us because it is written: Everyone who is hung on a tree is cursed. The purpose was that

the blessing of Abraham would come to the Gentiles by Christ Jesus so that we could receive the promised Spirit through faith."

God/Jesus/Holy Spirit loves you as if you are the only person on earth. When you pray, you do not take time away from others who may have "more important" issues. God wants to hear from you daily and has solutions for your everyday problems. God is in you and is in all believers. God is not confined to a 24-hour time clock. If you take an hour of God's time, that same hour is still available for everyone else on earth. He is available 24/7 for every believer. He is your personal Savior waiting to hear from you each day. How often do you want to hear from someone you love? That's how often God wants to hear from you!

John 15:13 HCSB

____

____

____

____

Everything contained in the current canon (compilation of sacred books) is enough information to make the case for faith in the Godhead. The writings included are agreed to be divinely-inspired and sufficient for faith.

Many writings did not make it into the current canon of the Bible. These other writings include fifty-four "apocryphal" texts (ancient texts written around the time 200 BCE - 100 CE), and are excluded from the Bible. Other writings are not required for faith and have been omitted due to doubtful authorship, questionable authenticity, outright Gnostic, Arian, or other non-Christian beliefs (heresy) and/or not considered to be divinely inspired.

John 21:25 NIV "Jesus did many other things as well. If every one

of them were written down, I suppose that even the whole world would not have room for the books that would be written."

PERSONAL REFLECTION:
HOW IS HOLY SPIRIT SPEAKING TO YOU THROUGH THESE SCRIPTURES?

____

____

____

____

ANSWER KEY LESSON 5.1: THE BIBLE: GOD'S WORD

2 Timothy 3:16 HCSB "All Scripture is inspired by God and is profitable for teaching, for rebuking, for correcting, for training in righteousness."

Romans 2:15 NLT "They demonstrate that God's law is written in their hearts, for their conscience and thoughts either accuse them or tell them they are doing right."

John 15:13 HCSB "No one has greater love than this, that someone would lay down his life for his friends."

LESSON 5.2

THE BIBLE: GOD'S WORD PT2

In this chapter, you find the answers to some common Biblical questions, but first, see if you can find God, Jesus, and Holy Spirit all in **Genesis 1**, the first book of the Bible.

Where do you first see God in the Bible?

Genesis 1:1 HCSB "In the beginning God created the heavens and the earth."

Where do you first see the Holy Spirit in the Bible?

Genesis 1:2 HCSB "Now the earth was formless and empty, darkness covered the surface of the watery depths, and the Spirit of God was hovering over the surface of the waters."

Where do you first see Jesus in the Bible?

Genesis 1:26 HCSB "Then God said, "Let Us make man in Our image, according to Our likeness."

Compare the 1st line of the Old Testament Genesis with the 1st line of the New Testament Gospel of John.

Genesis 1:1 HCSB "In the beginning God (Jesus/Holy Spirit) created the heavens and the earth."

John 1:1-3 HCSB "In the beginning was the Word (Jesus), and the Word (Jesus) was with God, and the Word (Jesus) was God. He (Jesus) was with God in the beginning. All things were created through Him (Jesus), and apart from Him (Jesus), not one thing was created that has been created."

Colossians 1:16 HCSB "For everything was created by Him (God/Jesus/Holy Spirit), in heaven and on earth, the visible and the invisible, whether thrones or dominions or rulers or authorities all things have been created through Him and for Him (God/Jesus/Holy Spirit)."

God communicates with us in numerous ways but primarily through the Holy Spirit in us and the Word of God, which is the teachings of Jesus in the Bible. We learn His "voice" when we meditate on His word.

John 10:27 HCSB

____

____

____

____

Why are there so many versions and translations of the Bible?

First, you should know that the Bible is the best-selling book in the world. It exceeds every book on the New York Times bestseller list every month, so they don't even include it in their listing. The Bible has sold over 5 billion copies and sells over six books every 10 seconds worldwide. It has been translated into over 3600 languages, including about 300 English versions.

Before we look at the various English versions, Concordance can be helpful for deeper Bible study. It will help you look up every word and every verse with Greek and Hebrew meanings so you can understand Scripture better and find parallel themes. There are free online Concordance apps that can make deep study easier.

For example, did you know that Jesus never used the word "love?" That's because Jesus did not speak English! He used Ahab in Hebrew and in Greek; Philia (Love of Friend), Eros (Love of Spouse), Storge (Empathetic Love), and Agape (Love of God) which are all different words for "love" with different meanings. You can see that Greek (in some cases) is much richer or may have a slightly different meaning than English translations. However, the word "love" sufficiently carries the meaning, and the message is not lost in translation to English. You can use Concordance when you're wanting to search for deeper meaning. The rest of the time, use several Bible versions and translations to better understand a passage's intent.

Here's a little experiment. Imagine for a moment that the original Scripture was written in French. You've been hired as a Biblical Scholar to translate a common French word to English without losing the original meaning.

Jesus said, "I'm having a little déjà vu here." Translate "déjà vu" into English.

____

____

____

____

Your translation of the word "déjà vu" might be "thought for thought", "word for word" or "paraphrased" but the meaning of the message would not be lost.

Déjà vu; The **thought for thought** translation is "to feel like you've already experienced something." The literal **word for word** translation (from French) is "already seen." Here are some different English translations.

TYPES OF BIBLE TRANSLATIONS

WORD FOR WORD

INTERLINEAR

AMP Amplified

NASB New American Standard Bible

ESV English Standard Version

RSV Revised Standard Version

KJV King James Version

NKJV New King James Version

THOUGHT FOR THOUGHT

CSB Christian Standard Bible

HCSBHolman Christian Standard Bible

NRSV New Revised Standard Version

NAB New American Bible

NET New English Translation

NIV New International Version

NLT New Living Translation

TNIV Today's New International Version

NCV New Century Version

PARAPHRASE

NIRV New International Reader's Version

GNT Good News Translation

CEV Contemporary English Version

TLB The Living Bible

MSG The Message Bible

PASSION

This is by no means a complete list. Www.BibleGateway.com offers 64 versions in English and more in Spanish.

Examples of Mark 16:15 in various translations from Greek:

(Literal Strong's Lexicon Concordance "to say, to go, all the whole, order the world, to be a herald/proclaim, good news, all every, creation/creature."

Word for word KJV "And he said unto them, Go ye into all the world, and preach the gospel to every creature."

Thought for thought NLT "And then he told them, Go into all the world and preach the Good News to everyone."

Paraphrased MSG "Then he said, Go into the world. Go everywhere and announce the Message of God's good news to one and all."

The (NLT) New Living Translation is a good translation for beginners looking for a Bible that is easy to read. It is a good balance of readability and accuracy to the original text. I've used several translations and versions in writing this book so you can get accustomed to the various expressions used in translation.

Depending on the reader's purpose, various translations and versions may be more helpful than others. A formal word-for-word equivalent may be preferred for teaching and preaching, while a functional thought-for-thought might be preferred for readability and understanding.

2 Timothy 3:16-17 HCSB "All Scripture is inspired by God and is profitable for teaching, for rebuking, for correcting, for training in righteousness, so that the man of God may be complete, equipped for every good work."

John 8:31-32 HCSB "So Jesus said to the Jews who had believed Him, "If you continue in My word, you are My disciples. You will know the truth, and the truth will set you free."

John 14:23 HCSB

____

____

____

____

The Bible reveals God's heart for humankind by sending Jesus to redeem us and provide a way to receive salvation even while we were still sinners. He speaks to you through His Word, the Bible. Meditate on each word, each verse, each chapter. Don't read it like a novel. Don't rush through it. Let it speak to you and apply it to your life. Let it wash over and transform you into the person Jesus called you to be. Enjoy God's presence while reading His Holy Word given to you.

PERSONAL REFLECTION:
HOW IS HOLY SPIRIT SPEAKING TO YOU THROUGH THESE SCRIPTURES?

ANSWER KEY LESSON 5.2: THE BIBLE: GOD'S WORD PT2

John 10:27 HCSB "My sheep listen to my voice; I know them, and they follow me."

John 14:23 HCSB Jesus replied, "Anyone who loves me will obey my teaching. My Father will love them, and we will come to them and make our home with them."

LESSON 6.1

PRAYER and WORSHIP

The Biblical Greek word for "church" is "ekklesia" and means "an assembly of people" coming together for Godly praise/worship and prayer.

No matter what church or denomination you belong to, Scripture tells us not to give up meeting together **(Hebrews 10:25)** even if it's just two or three people meeting in his name. **(Matthew 18:20).**

Prayer and Worship are closely related. There are several different kinds of prayers, one of which is a worship-style prayer of praise, adoration, and thanksgiving. Verbally recognizing the Lord's power, mercy, love, and other characteristics that you admire and adore is a wonderful way to pray.

A second type of prayer is lament and petition. God wants you to pray without ceasing **(1 Thessalonians 5:17)**, so there may be times when you may want to speak out the desires of your heart. This is verbalizing what's bothering you. Remember to speak words of faith. God knows your needs but wants to have a conversation with you. A good way to see God's hand in your life is to write down these petitions with the date of the prayer and the date it is answered. Before long you'll have a book of answered prayers

Intercession is a type of prayer that can be for yourself or others. Are there dangerous or difficult situations that need prayer? Requests made to God in these areas are very powerful and you can see God move in the results. These prayers come from the depth of your being and acknowledge our total dependence on God.

Healing and deliverance are closely related prayers. Whether an illness is planted by demons or a result of a virus or injury the prayer is the same to deliver someone back to wholeness and healing. The next chapter covers this prayer in more depth.

Prayers for guidance and wisdom are some of the most common and misused prayers. If you are going to pray for guidance, have enough wisdom to truly seek his answer, and have scripture to stand on before moving forward. He has better plans for you than you have for yourself.

That is by no means a comprehensive list, but it gives you an idea of the types of prayers people bring before the Lord.

Not all prayers must start with "Heavenly Father" and end "in Jesus' name." Just the word "Jesus" is a prayer by itself. "Breath Prayers" are very effective in bringing you into the presence of God and calming your mind. Breathe in and pray, "Jesus." Breathe out and pray, "You are wonderful." You can use any combination of one to two words while you breathe in and out.

Breath prayers are a simple way to prepare your mind for meditation on scripture or an effective way to connect with God. Start with a breath prayer. Close your eyes and picture Jesus in the room. Once you've located him, keep your eyes on Him, stop the meditation, quiet your mind, and let him minister to you. You might ask him a question in this state of devotion. "God is there anything you want to say to me? Do you have any instructions for me? Is there anything you want me to change?"He will speak to you with your quieted mind focused on him. He may speak to you in a small voice from inside you, thoughts or visions. The more you do this, the more you will hear and recognize

God's voice, even in a crowd with your eyes open.

Prayer is a form of communication between God and people that builds the relationship. Relationships flourish through effective communication. The quality of communication directly impacts the strength of the relationship. Every day that you don't pray, you are effectively telling God, "I don't need you today." Communication is a two-way process that includes both talking and listening. We talk to Him through prayer and worship. We listen to Him through meditation, a quiet mind, and Scripture. He speaks to us in many ways but primarily through His Word. We speak to Him in many ways, including prayer and worship, but our actions and intentions speak louder than words.

SCRIPTURE MEMORIZATION

Philippians 4:6-7 NIV "Do not be anxious about anything, but in every situation, by prayer and petition, with thanksgiving, present your requests to God. And the peace of God, which transcends all understanding, will guard your hearts and your minds in Christ Jesus."

Jesus said this about prayer.

Matthew 6:5-8 NIV "And when you pray, do not be like the hypocrites, for they love to pray standing in the synagogues and on the street corners to be seen by others. Truly I tell you, they have received their reward in full. But when you pray, go into your room, close the door, and pray to your unseen Father. Then your Father, who sees what is done in secret, will reward you. And when you pray, do not keep on babbling like pagans, for they think they will be heard because of their many words. Do not be like them, for your Father knows what you need before you ask him."

In **Matthew 6:9-13** the disciples were taught "The Lord's Prayer". This is a starting point and a very good template for prayer. However, all of the tenets of this prayer were fulfilled at the cross. For example: "**Our**

Father which art in heaven" has also made his home in you. He is not far from you in heaven. He is in you and your home is with him in heaven. There is no distance when you pray "Our Father who art in heaven." That this prayer starts with "Our Father", identifying God as "Father" is important even today.

"Thy kingdom come. Thy will be done." His kingdom has already come and walked among us. When Jesus said, **"The kingdom of God is at hand,"** he was talking about himself. **Luke 17:21 NLT "For indeed, the kingdom of God is within you."** God's will was done by Jesus, and it's up to us to enforce it. It's a good starting point if you know we are not waiting for him to do his will. He is waiting for us to do his will.

"Give us this day our daily bread." Our daily bread "is Jesus" and we have his fullness in us. **(John 6:35**). Jesus is the bread of life. It's up to us to partake in the daily bread by reading his word and spending time with Jesus. **"And forgive our trespasses."** 100% of our trespasses were forgiven at the cross. Are you getting this? It may be cathartic to pray for forgiveness because we occasionally fall short, but there's a part we do and a part God does. He has already forgiven us, so it's time to forgive yourself (and others), then renew your mind through thanksgiving that you were totally forgiven at the cross and walk again in our new identity and in the newness of life.

So, what can we glean from the Lord's prayer? It's exactly how the disciples needed to pray before the cross; the template still holds extreme value. Therefore, how shall we pray? Start with worship and thanksgiving. "Father, Hallowed be thy name!" Thank him for loving you and forgiving you. Honor, value and thank him for your many blessings. Worship and sing songs of praise. Find Scripture to stand on and pray accordingly. If it helps you to begin by praying the Lord's Prayer, do so to bring you into a deeper contemplative prayer that acknowledges that He is already present in you, you are already forgiven. You have a part in his will being done on earth as it is in heaven. The Kingdom, the

Power, and His Glory are already in you. (See **John 17:20-23** below.)

Before the cross, Jesus taught the Lord's Prayer in **Matthew 6:9-13**. Then Jesus prayed for people who would believe in him after his resurrection. This is how he prayed;

John 17:20-23 HCSB (Jesus speaking): "I pray not only for these, but also for those who believe in Me through their message. May they all be one, as You, Father, are in Me, and I am in You. May they also be one in Us, so the world may believe You sent Me. I have given them the glory You have given Me. May they be one as We are one. I am in them and You are in Me. May they be made completely one, so the world may know You have sent Me and have loved them as You have loved Me."

What happens when prayer seems not to be answered? God says "Ask" (**Matthew 7:7-11**), so we ask in prayer. Then we believe we have received the answer. **Mark 11:24. NIV "Whatever you ask for in prayer, believe that you have received it, and it will be yours."** God may answer in the spiritual realm or differently than you expected, but he always answers. By faith, you bring spiritual answers into physical manifestation. If God has to work through others to answer the prayer (for finances, for example), it could take longer for the others to respond. Pray that the others will hear from God and do the right thing to affect the answer. God always answers prayers, prayed in faith and according to his word. Remember that once you pray the focus becomes thanksgiving that God has already met our need.

1 John 5:14-15 NIV "This is the confidence we have in approaching God: that if we ask anything according to his will, he hears us. And if we know that he hears us—whatever we ask—we know that we have what we asked of him."

Prayers are effective. They can change circumstances. The sick can be made well, and finances can improve. Prayer can also affect atmospheres and outcomes according to His will. Prayer can do anything

God can do. Evil spirits must obey the prayers of a righteous person. And who is covered in Jesus's Righteousness? You are!

James 5:16 NIV "Confess your sins to each other and pray for each other so that you may be healed. The prayer of a righteous person is powerful and effective."

When it comes to prayer, Pastors, Priests, Elders, Deacons, and those who have passed on before us (including Saints) do not carry more power or authority than any other Christian. There is only one mediator between us and God, and it's none of the above. God is in you, and He has no favorites. God is not busy with "more important things" than hearing your direct prayers. Those who think they need a mediator other than Jesus do not believe Scripture.

1 Timothy 2:5 NIV “For there is one God, and one mediator between God and men, the man Christ Jesus.”

It's wonderful to have others pray for you or agree with you in prayer. Corporate prayer can be very effective.

Acts 12:5-7 NIV “So Peter was kept in prison, but the church was earnestly praying to God for him. The night before Herod was to bring him to trial, Peter was sleeping between two soldiers, bound with two chains, and sentries stood guard at the entrance. Suddenly an angel of the Lord appeared and a light shone in the cell. He struck Peter on the side and woke him up. "Quick, get up!" he said, and the chains fell off Peter's wrists.”

Matthew 18:19 NIV

____

____

____

____

Ephesians 1:18 NIV "I pray that the eyes of your heart may b enlightened so that you may know the hope to which he has call you, the riches of his glorious inheritance in his Holy people."

Ephesians 3:16-19 NIV "I pray that out of his glorious riches, may strengthen you with power through his Spirit in your inn being, so that Christ may dwell in your hearts through faith. A I pray that you, being rooted and established in love, may ha power, together with all the Lord's holy people, to grasp how w and long and high and deep is the love of Christ and to know t love that surpasses knowledge—that you may be filled to measure of all the fullness of God."

Other prayers Paul prayed for you in Scripture are found in **Ph pians 1:9-11 and Colossians 1:9-12.**

Jesus showed us the importance of prayer. Besides having a passio doing the will of His Father, making a way through him for all pe healing the sick, and casting out demons, he demonstrated the in tance of prayer. It was central to his ministry. In Scripture yo Jesus spending long hours day and night in prayer. While others sleeping, chasing their dreams, and distracted by the world, h fasting and praying.

PERSONAL REFLECTION:
HOW IS HOLY SPIRIT SPEAKING TO YOU THROUGH THESE SCRIPTURES?

____

____

____

____

ANSWER KEY LESSON 6.1: PRAYER AND WORSHIP

Hebrews 10:25 NIV "Do not giving up meeting together, as some are in the habit of doing, but encouraging one another—and all the more as you see the Day approaching."

Matthew 18:20 NIV "For where two or three gather in my name, there am I with them."

1 Thessalonians 5:17 NKJV "Pray without ceasing."

Matthew 18:19 NIV "Again, truly I tell you that if two of you on earth agree about anything they ask for, it will be done for them by my Father in heaven."

Philippians 1:9-11 NIV "And this is my prayer: that your love may abound more and more in knowledge and depth of insight so that you may be able to discern what is best and may be pure and blameless for the day of Christ, filled with the fruit of righteousness that comes through Jesus Christ—to the glory and praise of God."

Colossians 1:9-12 NIV "For this reason, since the day we heard about you, we have not stopped praying for you. We continually ask God to fill you with the knowledge of his will through all the wisdom and understanding that the Spirit gives, so that you may live a life worthy of the Lord and please him in every way: bearing fruit in every good work, growing in the knowledge of God, being strengthened with all power according to his glorious might so that you may have great endurance and patience, and giving joyful thanks to the Father, who has qualified you to share in the inheri-tance of his holy people in the kingdom of light."

LESSON 6.2

FAITH for YOURSELF and OTHERS

Now that you have the power of the Holy Spirit that raised Jesus from the dead living inside you, you have the power to raise others from the dead! What's more powerful; God or Medicine? What's more powerful; God or Cancer? Want to hear God laugh? Tell him you or someone you know has an "incurable disease." What's more difficult for God: Raising someone from the dead or curing infirmity?

John 14:12 NIV "Very truly I tell you, whoever believes in me will do the works I have been doing, and they will do even greater things than these because I am going to the Father."

God created everything by speaking. The power for faith to change circumstances is in the tongue. What you say about yourself has resulted in your current circumstances. Faith becomes effective when you speak life over yourself and others.

James 5:14-15 NKJV "Is anyone among you sick? Let him call for the elders of the church, and let them pray over him, anointing him with oil in the name of the Lord. And the prayer of faith will save the sick, and the Lord will raise him up."

The word "save" in this verse comes from the Greek word "sozo," which means "to save from suffering/disease, to make well, to heal and restore to health, healing in their body, wholeness."

Supernatural divine healing is available to all Christians. It is part of the atonement and what Jesus did for us at the cross. At the cross, Jesus put forgiveness of sins and healing in your bank account. Many people withdraw forgiveness of sin from their spiritual bank account but don't withdraw their healing. Both are in the atonement and both are available through faith.

1 Peter 2:24 NIV "He bore our sins in his body on the cross, so that we might die to sin and live for righteousness and by his wounds you have been healed."

Most churches don't have a supernatural group. They have men's and women's groups, bible study, recovery, singles, youth, etc., but few have a group dedicated to winning the lost and the subject of divine healing or the supernatural. It could be because someone prayed one time (or for years), and nothing happened. It's easier to point the finger at God and say, "It's not God's timing" or "God is allowing suffering to draw you closer to Him." Both of these statements are completely false. While physical suffering can draw you closer to God, He is love and He wants nothing but the best for you. **(Jeremiah 29:11).** While you can draw closer to God through infirmity, it is never God's will that you be sick. "Suffering" for God in the Bible always refers to "persecution," not illness.

For years, I prayed and got few results. After praying, "God, please heal this person," I heard in my spirit, "I won't answer that prayer. I gave all authority in heaven and on earth to Jesus."

Matthew 28:18 NIV (Jesus speaking) "All authority in heaven and on earth has been given to me."

So, I changed my prayer to, "Jesus, please heal this person." And I heard, "I won't answer that prayer. I put the Holy Spirit in you with all the power of the Godhead, who heals all illness and disease." I was praying wrong, and prayers were not being answered. I also wrongly blamed God. So, with my new biblical understanding and without any extra faith, I simply changed my prayer and started seeing healings and miracles. (Prayer for healing or deliverance is below in this chapter.)

Luke 10:17 NIV "Even Demons obey us when we use your name."

You have the authority to use the name of Jesus. When you speak, Jesus is speaking.

John 14:13 NIV "Whatever you ask in my name I will do that the Father may be glorified." (also John 15:16, John 16:23)

So why doesn't Jesus answer every prayer we pray in His name? First, the prayer must be backed by faith to be answered.

Matthew 21:22 NIV

____

____

____

____

Mark 11:24 NIV "Therefore I tell you, whatever you ask for in prayer, believe that you have received it and you will have it."

The person being prayed for does not need any faith. The person can be an atheist, Muslim, or of any other faith or of no faith. How much faith did Lazurus have when Jesus prayed him back from the dead? None. He was dead. How many Christians did Jesus pray for? None. (although some were followers they were not called Christians until after Jesus's death.)

If a person has any faith, they can add it to yours. Their doubt does not affect the result of your prayer. You carry enough faith for both. As you pray for others and see results, your faith will grow with more power for greater results. You have to learn to trust God.

Any prayer that includes “if it be your will” is prayed in doubt that its God's will to heal, and will not be answered. Jesus healed EVERYONE that asked. It is ALWAYS His will to heal. Besides praying wrong and with doubt, another reason for the lack of results is that you don't know the Scripture you are standing on. For example: "I pray that my team wins the game." God has no favorites so he will not answer this prayer. There is no Scripture you can stand on for your team to win the game.

Romans 2:11 NIV “God does not show favoritism.”

Prayer is very powerful when you know what Scripture backs up your prayer. For example: Lord, you said in **Mark 16:18 (paraphrased) that "if we lay hands on the sick, they will recover."** You can expect this prayer to be answered.

Mark 16:18 NIV “And these signs will accompany those who believe: In my name, they will drive out demons; they will speak in new tongues; they will pick up snakes with their hands; and when they drink deadly poison, it will not hurt them at all; they will place their hands on sick people, and they will get well.”

People may point to unforgiveness as a hindrance to prayer. **Mark 11:25 (paraphrased) "When you stand praying, forgive others."** It's a good practice to always forgive and keep the slate clean before man and God, but since this requirement is in **Mark** and not in the New Testament (after Jesus's death), your sin of unforgiveness was taken care of at the cross, even unforgiveness does not hinder your prayers.

The only other thing found in the New Testament that may be a hindrance to prayer is in **1 Peter 3:7 (paraphrased) "Husbands must honor their wives…treat her as you should so your prayers will not be hindered."** This not only applies to husbands but also to wives.

Your faith increases when you practice it. When you know Jesus and trust his word, you can have faith for yourself and others.

2 Corinthians 5:7 NIV

____

____

MEMORIZATION VERSE

Hebrews 11:1 NIV "Now faith is the substance of things hoped for, the evidence of things not seen."

Faith is drawn from the knowledge of God and it starts in the spiritual realm.

1 Corinthians 2:1 NIV "Your faith should not stand in the wisdom of men but in the power of God."

We use our five physical senses, sight, touch, hearing, smell, and taste, to grasp the things of men. When we add the spiritual sense of faith, we can begin to tap into seeing, feeling, hearing, smelling, and tasting in the spiritual realm. If you have "heard" from the Holy Spirit without hearing an audible voice you are beginning to understand the concept of spiritual senses. God will "touch" you without a physical sensation. **"Taste and see that the Lord is good." NIV Psalm 34:8**, etc. You can develop your physical senses into spiritual senses.

In the past, you may have been the one calling others to pray for you. As you practice what you've learned in this book, your faith will grow, and you will be the one people call for prayer.

Often, people will need prayer for depression, injury, or illness. Sometimes, the enemies of God (devils/demons, evil spirits, etc.) will have left the seeds of affliction or may still be tormenting the person you are praying for in their sleep or daily thoughts. The prayer is the same whether it's a demon you are casting out or a physical injury.

Jesus spent a significant amount of time casting out demons, healing the sick, and doing miracles. Remember to believe that the person has already received healing at the cross. Jesus took our infirmity and our diseases.

Matthew 8:17 NIV "He took up our infirmities and bore our diseases."

Also, remember that we now live by faith and not by sight. (**2 Corinthians 5:7**). No matter what you are looking at, see the person as healed and whole. The way Jesus sees them in heaven. You are bringing God to them, not them to God. You have the answer to prayer because you carry God in you. You represent Jesus with Holy Ghost power. We are not asking God to heal them. God told you to heal them and he gave you the power of the Holy Spirit and the authority of Jesus' name to do it!

Before you pray, ask the pain level from 1-10 in the person so they can take an assessment and know if anything has changed after prayer.

THE PRAYER FOR HEALING/DELIVERANCE in your own words will go something like this: "Thank you, Father, for this divine appointment. By the power of the Holy Spirit that raised Jesus from the dead and lives in me, I command all illness to leave (NAME) now in Jesus's name. I speak to the (specific illness/disease or injured part of the body) and call you healed right now. All pain and discomfort must leave now. Healing flow from the top of their head to the soles of their feet. Body be healed right now in Jesus' name."

Ask them to do something they couldn't do before. Reassess. Get the new pain level. Pray a second or third time as long as they still need improvement. Miracles happen instantly. Healing can start immediately but may take a day, a week, or longer. Keep this person in your prayers for the next few days. See them healed in the Spirit.

There are many courses that teach Divine healing, and many books have been written on this subject, but even with this simple prayer and the faith you already have, you will begin to see results. When you step out in faith, God will meet you there. There is a part you do and a part God does. Give God a platform so he can do his part. Pray for others!

If the person you are praying for says the pain is worse or the pain has moved or begins to manifest in a tormented way, then you are likely dealing with a demonic spirit. Continue the prayer as above or you may want to add Scripture like **Philippians 2:9-10 NIV "At the name of Jesus every knee shall bow in heaven, on earth and under the earth and every tongue will confess that Jesus is Lord."**

After reciting **Philippians 2:9-10** or other scripture, just say in your own words, "By the power of the Holy Spirit in me, I command all unclean spirits to leave him/her now in the name of Jesus." Pray this over and over again until the person is free. The only weapon Jesus used to defeat Satan was the word of God. When you use His name demons must obey.

Movies have inflated the power and authority of Satan and demons, but Scripture is clear. The only power Satan has is deception. He has no power or authority over you. Adam yielded authority to Satan but Jesus restored dominion over all the earth to us. We have been given the power of the Holy Spirit and the authority to use the name of Jesus to enforce what Jesus has already done. Satan can't do anything unless you give him access to do it.

Mark 16:17 NIV "And these signs will follow the believer; In my name, they will cast out demons; they will speak with new tongues."

Satan's major lie is that whatever your weakness is, "just one more time will fulfill your desire forever." You can quit after "just one more time." "No one will know." "You aren't hurting anyone." Sin opens the door for Satan to have access into your life. A foothold becomes a stronghold. God has done His part. He has defeated Satan and put power in you, not just to overcome the temptation but to eliminate the desire to ever sin again.

James 4:7 NIV

____

____

Romans 13:14 NIV "Clothe yourselves with the Lord Jesus Christ and do not think about how to gratify the desires of the flesh."

John 10:10 NIV "The thief comes only to steal and kill and destroy, but I have come that they may have life, and have it to the full."

1 Peter 5:8 NIV "Satan prowls around looking for those who will leave a sinful door open so he can destroy finances, relationships, and health."

God didn't just give authority to a few Pastors. He gave ALL OF US ALL AUTHORITY AND DOMINION to prowl around to save, heal, and set people free! He is looking for regular Christians to step into their new identity!

MEMORIZATION VERSE

Hebrews 11:1 NIV "Now faith is confidence in what we hope for and assurance about what we do not see."

PERSONAL REFLECTION:
HOW IS HOLY SPIRIT SPEAKING TO YOU THROUGH THESE SCRIPTURES?

____

____

____

____

ANSWER KEY LESSON 6.2: FAITH FOR YOURSELF AND OTHERS

Jeremiah 29:11 NIV "For I know the plans I have for you," declares the LORD, "plans to prosper you and not to harm you, plans to give you hope and a future."

Matthew 21:22 NIV "If you have faith and do not doubt and if you believe, you will receive what you have asked for."

2 Corinthians 5:7 NIV "For we live by faith and not by sight."
James 4:7 NIV "Submit yourselves to God, resist the devil, and he will flee from you."

LESSON 7.1

DISCIPLESHIP and LEADERSHIP

Your love for God does not translate to being a Christian however you want to be. If you are comfortable in your Christianity, then it's probably time to ask God, "How can I grow?" This list might help identify some areas that God wants you to grow.

STAGES OF GROWTH IN CHRIST

Spiritually Dead.

Accept Jesus as Lord and Savior.

Baby Christian

Spiritual birth and learning your new identity in Christ.

Trust your life and death to Christ.

Eliminate foul language, lying, cheating, stealing, addictions, etc

Begin to prioritize prayer life.

Self-centered faith.

Young Christian

Start to donate time and money to the church.

Start to read scripture.

Give remaining bad habits to God.

Trade anxiety for faith and learn to trust God.

Eliminate anger and begin to enjoy the peace and joy of God.

Start to recognize and yield to the voice of the Holy Spirit.

Scripture memorization.

Mature Christian

Prioritize relationships: God, family, friends, and work.

Material things have less importance.

Daily Bible reading/study.

Teach, join/lead small groups.

Serving in and giving to the Church.

Use gifts of the Spirit; Wisdom, Faith, Healing, Prophesy, etc.

Elder

Walk by faith and not by sight or circumstances.

Found the joy of serving, giving/finances, fasting, and prayer.

Walk like Jesus. Love God and others is a top priority.

Others-centered faith. Lead prayer for others.

Live out the Great Commission. Get others saved, set free, healed.

Exemplify fruits of the Spirit: love, peace, patience, kindness, etc.

Hearing God more clearly. Obeying the Holy Spirit.

Discipling others.

In **Acts 11:26**, the disciples were first called "Christians." The nouns "disciple" and "Christian" are interchangeable in the New Testament. What does biblical "discipleship" mean then? It means bringing people to Christ and growing them into mature believers. There is no limit to the number of ways to do this. It is as varied as your personality. In the next section, you will learn a simple way to start the conversation with pre-Christians. "Pre-Christian" is a hopeful term used for anyone who is not a "born-again believer" yet.

The New Testament gives us some suggestions. (All Paraphrased)

Titus 2:4 Older women are to train younger women.

2 Timothy 2:2 Paul trained Timothy to train others to train others.

Ephesians 6:4 Fathers are to train their children.

Matthew 28:20 Missionaries are to train the nations.

Hebrews 3:13 All Christians should build each other up for love and good works.

1 Peter 4:10 All Christians are to use their gifts to serve others.

Every Christian should grow and share the Good News of Christ with pre-Christians, and help other believers grow. Discipleship includes discipling and also being discipled. We should never stop growing into the likeness of Jesus. Many Christians live lukewarm lives. They read the Bible, pray, and fast in their prayer rooms, possibly even hours per day, but this is only step one. This is a safe Christianity that closes doors and no longer seeks to save the lost. Lukewarm Christianity concentrates on self.

We need to move beyond being baby Christians. Our love for God needs to transition to love for pre-Christians. Being about Father's business means getting his people saved, healed, and delivered and encountering His power in our daily walk. It means living with intentionality in our new identity and doing the work of the Gospel.

This book is about equipping new believers. It has laid out what Jesus did for us and what he asked us to do in return. Have you ever noticed that people ALWAYS make time for the things they love to do? God loves you. He sent his son to die for you. How much time do you have for Him? He has nothing but time for you 24/7. He's not too busy with more important things. You are the most important thing to Him.

What do you love more than God and make time for daily; movies, reading, games, apps, sports, the news? Have you ever noticed that people talk most about the things they love; children, grandchildren, hobbies, etc.? This may be harsh, but if you aren't talking about Jesus, he's probably not high on your love list. If you are not making daily time for Him, he's probably not a priority. I'll use the example of someone you love. Are they on your mind often during the day? Do you look forward to their call? Is spending time with them a priority? This is how Jesus feels about you. How do you feel about Him?

Jesus calls us to "go and make disciples of all nations." “Nations” starts with the people around you. This command drove early followers of Christ into a strategic mission that transformed the world. They accomplished this not only by sharing the Gospel but also by training new believers. To be a Christian is to be a disciple and be a disciple-maker.

Matthew 28:20 NLT “Teach these new disciples to obey all the commands I have given you. And be sure of this: I am with you always, even to the end of the age."

The commands are to love God and love others. How do we love God and love others? By sharing the Gospel (Good News) and getting people born-again and discipled.

James 1:22 NIV "But don't just listen to God's word. You must do what it says. Otherwise, you are only fooling yourselves."

Luke 6:47-48 NIV "Everyone who comes to Me and hears My words and acts on them, I will show you whom he is like: he is like a man building a house, who dug deep and laid a foundation on the rock; and when a flood occurred, the torrent burst against that house and could not shake it, because it had been well built."

Jesus compares those who put His words into practice to those who have dug deep and laid a foundation on the rock. When you begin to disciple someone you have the opportunity to help them lay the foundation for a love relationship with God.

1 Corinthians 11:1 NLT

____

____

____

____

Luke 6:40 NLT "Students are not greater than their teacher. However, the student who is fully trained will become like the teacher."

We are called to a whole new life. We are not only forgiven of our sins; we are given new hearts designed to love God and others. Fulfilling this call fills the void that the things of the world can not fill.

You are the representative of Jesus and you are the Church.

If you don't pray, no one prays.

If you don't serve, no one serves.

If you don't read the Bible, no one reads the Bible.

If you don't go to church, no one goes to church.

If you don't bring unbelievers to Christ, no one gets saved.

If you don't get people healed supernaturally, no one gets healed supernaturally.

If you don't give, no one gives and the list goes on.

Again, you are the representative of Jesus and you are the Church.

Philippians 2:13 NLT

____

____

____

____

Mark 8:34 NLT "Then, calling the crowd to join his disciples, he said, "If any of you wants to be my follower, you must give up your way, take up your cross, and follow me."

Many Christians today associate "taking up your cross" with some type of suffering for Jesus. This is not true. While your friends and family may no longer recognize the new person you are becoming, "Taking up your cross" just means putting down your earthly priorities and taking up Kingdom priorities. It's the ultimate act of surrender. It's a conscious choice to deny yourself and live for Christ. It means a willingness to follow and obey Christ, not out of obligation but out of love for what He has done for you.

Discipleship is foundational to Christianity. To be a disciple is to follow Jesus, reach the lost, and engage in this process with other believers.

In the Gospel of **Matthew 25:14-30**, Jesus tells the parable of the talents. In the parable, the master gives his servants different amounts of talents (money) before going away. He trusts them to use these talents based on their ability. When he returns he judges them based on what they did with the gift he entrusted them with. The parable is a lesson on being responsible for the spiritual and physical resources He has given you. What have you done with the precious gift of the Holy Spirit?

Describe in your own words what you think it means to be a disciple.

____

____

____

____

____

____

____

____

____

____

PERSONAL REFLECTION:

HOW IS HOLY SPIRIT SPEAKING TO YOU THROUGH THESE SCRIPTURES?

____

____

____

____

ANSWER KEY LESSON 7.1: DISCIPLESHIP AND LEADERSHIP

1 Corinthians 11:1 NLT (Paul speaking) "And you should imitate me, just as I imitate Christ."

Philippians 2:13 NLT "It is God who works in you to will and to act in order to fulfill his good purpose."

Matthew 25:14-30 NLT "It will be like a man going on a journey, who called his servants and entrusted to them his property. To one he gave five talents, to another two, to another one, to each according to his ability. Then he went away. He who had received the five talents went at once and traded with them, and he made five talents more. So also he who had the two talents made two talents more. But he who had received the one talent went and dug in the ground and hid his master's money. Now after a long time the master of those servants came and settled accounts with them. And he who had received the five talents came forward...His master said to him, 'Well done, good and faithful servant. You have been faithful over a little; I will set you over much. Enter into the joy of your master.' And he also who had the two talents came forward...His master said to him, 'Well done, good and faithful servant. You have been faithful over a little; I will set you over much. Enter into the joy of your master.' He also who had received the one talent came forward, saying, 'Master... I was afraid, and I went and hid your talent in the ground. Here, you have what is yours.' But his master answered him, 'You wicked and slothful servant! You ought to have invested my money with the bankers, and at my coming I should have received what was my own with interest. So take the talent from him and give it to him who has the ten talents. For to everyone who has will more be given, and he will have an abundance. But from the one who has not, even what he has will be taken away. And he cast the worthless servant into the outer darkness."

LESSON 7.2

EVANGELISM

The First Commission was given in **Genesis** to Adam.

Genesis 1:28 NLT "Then God blessed them and said, "Be fruitful and multiply. Fill the earth and govern it. Reign over the fish in the sea, the birds in the sky, and all the animals that scurry along the ground."

For those that think the earth is overpopulated, it is estimated that you could fit all the people on earth at the time of this writing (approx 8 billion people) into the State of Maine, USA, and give everyone approximately 124 sq ft.

The Commission in **Genesis** given to humanity has not changed. What changed is that the first man (Adam) gave his authority and dominion over to Satan when he sinned against God. From that time until Jesus (the second Adam) came, Satan ruled the earth. Jesus restored dominion to people at the cross and restores their relationship to God for all those who accept His gift.

With this restored status and new covenant Jesus issued a (new) Great Commission. It is found in **Matthew 28:16-20, Mark 16:15-18, Luke**

24:44-49, John 20:19-23, and Acts 1:8. Here is a paraphrased summary of the Great Commission found in the **Gospels** and **Acts**. God's instruction to His people is; **"I give you dominion over the earth (again). Now, go multiply, get people born-again/saved, healed/set free, baptized, and make disciples that make disciples telling of the Good News of God."**

No matter what your job is in or outside the church, whether you are President, Pastor, Teacher, Student, Janitor, or retired, and no matter what your natural or spiritual gift or calling is, God has given all people the same directive in the Great Commission.

Mark 16:15-18 NLT "He said to them, "Go into all the world and preach the gospel to all creation. Whoever believes and is baptized will be saved, but whoever does not believe will be condemned. And these signs will accompany those who believe: In my name, they will drive out demons; they will speak in new tongues; they will pick up snakes with their hands; and when they drink deadly poison, it will not hurt them at all; they will place their hands on sick people, and they will get well."

This is where 80% of Christians fail. We've read the Scriptures and believe in God/Jesus/Holy Spirit. He has a specific calling given to ALL Christians to go get people born-again and to make disciples but most will stop at the "knowing" and never step into the "doing." Those who "do" will point to their specific calling as teacher, preacher, or other service but miss the greater calling given to all Christians (make disciples). Some may even hide behind their service role or become very busy serving but will never turn to the task Jesus gave us of "fishing for people."

Matthew 4:19 NLT "Jesus called out to them, "Come, follow me, and I will show you how to fish for people!"

It is estimated that less than 5% of Christians will lead another person to Christ in their lifetime. This does not mean inviting someone to church. It means sharing the Gospel in a way that leads someone to come to faith in Jesus. We can't hide behind our "job" and say that the great commission "is not for me." When God tells you to do something, he gives you the tools, power, and boldness to do it.

2 Timothy 1:7 NLT "For God has not given us a spirit of timidity but of power and love and discipline."

This book is designed to prepare the new believer to be activated into His Calling to share the Gospel. It has laid the groundwork for your new identity in Christ and a new understanding of your power to use all the tools God has given you. It was written to encourage lukewarm Christians, activate dead Christians, and bring pre-Christians into the Kingdom. Whatever someone needs, you carry the answer when you carry Jesus!

If you don't have a friend who understands the Gospel the way you do now, have them read this book and buddy up! It's time to become the person God created you to be and spread the Good News.

Here's a quick test to see if you are on task for God. How many people have you led to the Lord in the last year? How many have you discipled in the last month? How many have you prayed for in the last week?

My prayer each morning is, "God, Please put someone in my path who needs you today." Well, that's just about everyone. Then, as you go about your business expect God will make a divine appointment for you.

I was on vacation with a friend in North Carolina. After my morning prayer, we walked out of the hotel and on the way to breakfast across the street. Sitting on the curb in our path was a man. My friend and I were both hungry as we walked by. Then I remembered who I am, and whose I am. I remembered my primary mission. I walked over and asked the man if he had heard the Good News! He said what Good News? I said: Jesus loves you! He said Yes, I love Him too. Thinking my job was done I added; Is there anything I can pray for you about? He said his back pain was level ten and he could not stand up straight. I prayed and the man was instantly healed! Praise God! His pain level dropped from ten to zero and he stood up and walked straight. A template for healing prayer is in Chapter 6.2.

HERE'S A TEMPLATE FOR BRINGING PEOPLE TO CHRIST.

Have you heard the Good News? Jesus loves you.

Do you KNOW Jesus, or do you know ABOUT Jesus?

Jesus is not about religion or going to church.

Can I ask you a couple of questions?

Do you believe God created you for a relationship with him?

Do you believe sin messed up that relationship?

Jesus came to restore your relationship with God.

Would you like to accept this gift and make Jesus your Lord and Savior today?

Then lead them in the Prayer of Salvation in Chapter 1.1.

The prayer model above was learned at a BELONG Seminar at 33rd Company ministry in Ft Worth, Texas. I've learned a lot from Holy Spirit, Scripture, Seminary, Seminars, and studying the great Christian Generals of the past. My walk with Christ has been a work in process and a tapestry of influence from those who have walked in power and love before me. Your walk is likely the same. When you implement the teachings of Jesus, contained in Scripture you will begin to walk in a supernatural life that God has called you.

In my early walk with Jesus, I was afraid to even say to people, "Have a blessed day!" If someone had a problem, I would say, "My thoughts and prayers are with you." If someone needed prayer, I would tell them I would pray…later, of course. Sometimes I would pray, and sometimes I would forget. I never saw any healing or miracles in my feeble attempts. It wasn't until I started praying right when people said they needed prayer and changed my prayer to how Jesus prayed (Example in Chapter 6.2) that I started seeing better results.

Christianity is not something to do on Sundays. It's a lifestyle of supernatural occurrences as you yield your will to God's will, and grow up into him on this earth.

You are encouraged to begin to share your 1-2 minute personal testimony of what Jesus has done for you with others. If the circumstances don't allow a 2-minute testimony, the simple question; "Have you heard the Good News?" will open the conversation.

Remember that when you begin to share the Good News, it is no longer you speaking but God speaking through you. By beginning the conversation, you give God the platform for evangelism or healing. God does the rest.

It takes time and practice. You won't be perfect the first time, so don't be afraid to keep trying. Your love will minister to others even if you don't do everything perfectly. Begin ministering to others, recognizing that you are gifted by God. Share the supernatural abilities He has given you with other people.

Galatians 2:20 NIV "I have been crucified with Christ and I no longer live, but Christ lives in me. The life I now live in the body, I live by faith in the Son of God, who loved me and gave himself for me."

1 Peter 1:10-11 NIV "Therefore, my brothers and sisters, make every effort to confirm your calling and election. For if you do these things, you will never stumble, 11 and you will receive a rich welcome into the eternal kingdom of our Lord and Savior Jesus Christ."

Luke 4:18-21 NLT "The Spirit of the Lord is on me because he has anointed me to proclaim good news to the poor. He has sent me to

proclaim freedom for the prisoners and recovery of sight for the blind, to set the oppressed free, to proclaim the year of the Lord's favor."

We are Christ's body and represent Him in the world today. Jesus' mission is our mission. He has commanded us to share the Good News with everyone. Our task is to actively oppose the devil's work and enforce what Jesus has already done. When we proclaim the Gospel to those who are lost, God provides salvation, healing, forgiveness of sins, restoration to relationship with God, and dominion to His people.

WRITE YOUR 1 - 2 MINUTE TESTIMONY

____

____

____

____

____

____

____

____

____

____

____

____

____

____

____

____

____

____

____

____

ACTIVATION

1. Practice your testimony.
2. Practice leading someone to the Lord. (Template Chapter 7.2 and Prayer Chapter 1.1)
3. Practice words of knowledge and other gifts of the Spirit. (Gifts in Chapter 4.1)
4. Practice getting someone healed. (Prayer in Chapter 6.2)

Remember that all the power of the Holy Spirit in you is what you are activating. You are practicing your new identity by using the gifts you have been given. Signs and wonders while walking with God in supernatural power for the Great Commission await you along the way. God is with you.

We practice because no one was born in greatness. They practiced. If the first nine people are not healed when you pray, pray for the tenth. If the first nine people don't get born-again, present your testimony and the Gospel to the tenth. You may plant a seed, water or harvest. You do your part and God will do His.

Many Christians get this far and never step out on faith. They've never known the power of the Holy Spirit in them. They've never known the power of prayer that God promises for those who believe. I've heard "When I'm older, I'll take it more seriously." "Once I get things situated with school or work." "Once my finances are in order" or "when things settle down at home, then I'll be able to focus more on Spiritual matters and read my Bible." This attitude is out of alignment with God's best for your life. When you arrange your priorities with God first, family second, friends third, and work fourth (you can put "self" wherever you like except first), your life will start to align with what God has intended for you.

Christians who are inconsistent in their prayer life, in their worship, and in their devotion to the Word are more likely to experience stress and anxiety and be tossed around in the winds of change in their life. The Word is a firm foundation. God never changes and is always there for you. You can not hope to receive God's plan and protection in your life when you are drawn first to things of the world.

You may hear some Christians say "You must put the flesh to death" or "put the flesh down." What people are saying is when your soul attempts to take precedence over the spirit you become double-minded. This is more common with new believers, but as you live a life of faith, the Spirit in you helps you make single-minded choices that honor God. As you practice spiritual discipline, God can speak to you and through you and you will know his voice. Discipline starts when you shut off your phone, turn off the TV, put away the distractions (internal and external) then go to the Word and pray.

Spiritual discipline may start as a chore but becomes a place of solace, security, comfort, and peace and turns into a place of joy in the Lord. If you are missing true joy in your life, you are likely lacking spiritual discipline and seeking satisfaction from temporary (double-minded) worldly pleasures.

A supernatural (single-minded) life awaits when you practice the things God has shown you in Scripture and confirm in your spirit.

James 2:17 NLT "Faith by itself, if it is not accompanied by action, is dead."

James 1:7-8 NLT "Such people should not expect to receive anything from the Lord. Their loyalty is (double-minded) divided between God and the world, and they are unstable in everything they do."

Philippians 6:6 NLT "I pray that your partnership with us in the faith may be effective in deepening your understanding of every good thing we share for the sake of Christ."

FINAL MEDITATION

In my new understanding Father, I pray that
my eyes are your eyes, and your eyes are my eyes
so I can meet the needs of others,
my ears are your ears, and your ears are my ears
so I can hear the Holy Spirit's directions,
my feet are your feet, and your feet are my feet
so I walk is where you send me,
my heart is your heart, and your heart is my heart
so I can love others the way you do,
my mind is your mind, and your mind is my mind
so I may have wisdom in every situation,
and finally, my life is your life, and your life is my life
so God is glorified.

PERSONAL REFLECTION:
HOW IS HOLY SPIRIT SPEAKING TO YOU THROUGH THESE SCRIPTURES?

____

____

____

____

Made in the USA
Columbia, SC
18 September 2024